The

Whirlybird Anthology

of

Kansas City Writers

The
Whirlybird Anthology

of

Kansas City Writers

EDITED BY

VERNON ROWE, MARYFRANCES WAGNER

DAVID RAY, JUDY RAY

Whirlybird Press
Shawnee, Kansas

Front cover: Elizabeth Rowe, "The new Kansas City," 2012

The Kauffman Center for the Performing Arts opened in downtown Kansas City, Missouri, in September, 2011.

Back cover: Elizabeth Rowe, "J. C. Nichols Fountain," 2012

The fountain was created by sculptor Henri-Léon Gréber in Paris in 1910 for an estate in New York, moved to Kansas City, and dedicated at the Country Club Plaza in 1960.

Cover design by Tim Barnhart

Book design by Judy Ray

Acknowledgments appear on page 242 and following.

Library of Congress Control Number: 2012950279
First edition

ISBN: 978-0-9647053-6-4

Whirlybird Press
22052 W. 66th Street * Suite 342 * Shawnee * KS 66226

Preface

*Compose. (No ideas
but in things) Invent!*
— William Carlos Williams

Kansas City is big enough to do the civilized work of a city in higher education and promotion of the arts, yet small enough to have a root system in the culture and land around it. It is a place where the tectonic plates of Google and the Prairie meet. From this collision of major cultural forces come many little art-quakes, and occasionally a larger one.

Inspiration for compiling this anthology came during a workshop held at The Writers Place. As the participants and editors read and discussed poetry, they made note of earlier regional collections and a range of journals and other publications on the library shelves surrounding the group. It seemed time to recognize anew the vitality of Kansas City's literary scene. Whirlybird Press honors this rich traditional and ongoing cultural legacy.

Over the years, a great many writers have lived and worked in Kansas City, so this collection could not be comprehensive, and some fine submissions could not be included. But the plan has been to represent writers with pieces they considered their best short works. For deceased writers, the editors picked favorites.

In some of the selections Kansas City itself is subject or backdrop, for example when Richard Rhodes and Hilary Masters recall specifics of their childhood, or when David Owen returns to explore remembered odors, or when poets respond to the influences of jazz. But also found in these pages are subjects and styles as varied as can be imagined — and imagination is not bound by place.

The editors believe this collection will give readers everywhere an appreciation for some of the remarkable people who have made Kansas City their home. And we hope it will give sustenance to those writers who live here now and provide them with a sense of continuity with a well-honed literary tradition, to serve as a taproot through space and time.

*Vernon Rowe
October, 2012*

CONTENTS

Preface

Ernest Hemingway
Hilary Masters
Diane Glancy
Tina Hacker
Mbembe Milton Smith
Frank Higgins
Hadara Bar-Nadav
Robert Stewart

Mitrailliatrice

The mills of the gods grind slowly;
But this mill
Chatters in mechanical staccato.
Ugly short infantry of the mind,
Advancing over difficult terrain,
Make this Corona
Their mitrailleuse.

Montparnasse

There are never any suicides in the quarter among people one knows
No successful suicides.
A Chinese boy kills himself and is dead.
(they continue to place his mail in the letter rack at the Dome)
A Norwegian boy kills himself and is dead.
(no one knows where the other Norwegian boy has gone)
They find a model dead
alone in bed and very dead.
(it made almost unbearable trouble for the concierge)
Sweet oil, the white of eggs, mustard and water, soap suds
and stomach pumps rescue the people one knows.
Every afternoon the people one knows can be found at the café.

Champs d'Honneur

Soldiers never do die well;
    Crosses mark the places,
Wooden crosses where they fell;
    Stuck above their faces.
Soldiers pitch and cough and twitch;
    All the world roars red and black,
Soldiers smother in a ditch;
    Choking through the whole attack.

[Night comes with soft and drowsy plumes...]

Night comes with soft and drowsy plumes
To darken out the day
To stroke away the flinty glint
Softening out the clay
Before the final hardness comes
Demanding that we stay.

Captives

Some came in chains
Unrepentant but tired.
Too tired but to stumble.
Thinking and hating were finished
Thinking and fighting were finished
Retreating and hoping were finished.
Cures thus a long campaign,
Making death easy.

Riparto d'Assalto

Drummed their boots on the camion floor,
Hob-nailed boots on the camion floor.
Sergeants stiff,
Corporals sore.
Lieutenants thought of a Mestre whore —
Warm and soft and sleepy whore,
Cozy, warm and lovely whore:
Damned cold, bitter, rotten ride,
Winding road up the Grappa side.
Arditi on benches stiff and cold,
Pride of their country stiff and cold,
Bristly faces, dirty hides —
Infantry marches, Arditi rides.
Grey, cold, bitter, sullen ride —
To splintered pines on the Grappa side
at Asalone, where the truck-load died.

Schwarzwald

As white hairs in a silver fox's skin
The birches lie against the dark pine hill
They're talking German in the compartment
Now we're winding up
Through tunnels
Puffing
Dark valleys, noisy rivered
Rock filled, barred with white.
Heavy browed houses
Green fields,
Forested with hop poles
A flock of geese along the road.
I knew a gypsy once who said
He hoped to die here.

from *Last Stands: Notes from Memory*

My grandmother had found in the loam of Tom Pendergast's political machine a nourishment not supplied by the spare landscape my grandfather had transposed from the Montana of his army days. Her statuesque beauty, her soft, easygoing nature and graceful expression were great assets to the party and to its leaders, who were quick to use such natural gifts for their own ends. Her prominence in Church affairs, as president of the women's auxiliary of the Knights of Columbus, together with the associations she held as Capt. John Moynihan's daughter, presented the organization with a fabric of allegiances and goodwill already woven and ready to wear.

To be both Irish and a Democrat those early days in Kansas City was to be doubly punished, and to be a woman as well was to take that punishment into exile, but she must have sensed something was about to happen that would reverse this situation, some demographic shift that would alter the registration books and the voting slips, though she would never think of it in those terms but something more immediate, more personal, like a remembrance of her girlhood in the Bottoms, one of Capt. John Moynihan's three talented daughters, in the same neighborhood where the Pendergast brothers ran an honest saloon. She would make that connection, out of nostalgia, out of pride, out of self-preservation.

And it was a chance that paid off, beginning on the hot morning of April 10, 1930. According to the *Kansas City Journal-Post*, it was the hottest April 10th in forty-two years, 88° at one P.M., so that on that morning the council chamber in the old city hall was a blur of fans and programs, the air heated up even more by the klieg lights set up for motion-picture cameras, as a new mayor and city council were to be inaugurated, establishing another record: the first Democratic administration, mayor and city council, to be elected in Kansas City in living memory. Shoulder to shoulder the jammed crowd of loyal workers patiently followed the outgoing Republican mayor as he conducted the final business with the lame duck council; the programs and fans of the patient crowd worked the air, redolent with

4

sweat and the fragrance of the floral tributes, hundreds of dollars' worth of flowers banked on a temporary platform built at the end of the hall. The fans and programs worked as if the temperature of the day might conspire with the temper of the recent political debate to raise a heat that would melt the Democratic victory. Then, the mayor-elect entered, Bryce B. Smith, and the crowd stood and gave a great cheer.

> The youngest Democrat in the council chamber was Hillary [*sic*] Thomas Masters, 2-year-old son of Edgar Lee Masters, noted poet and author of New York. The child lives with his maternal grandmother, Mrs. T. F. Coyne, 3228 Roberts Street, an active Democratic worker. She had a seat just outside the railing of the room and little Hillary, dressed in a bright yellow suit, sat on the railing above the heads of most of the crowd and applauded vigorously every time his grandmother gave him the cue. He was the only child at the inaugural.

The only child at the inaugural, and dressed in a yellow suit, held high above the crowd, told when to applaud: a scene stealer, and meant to steal that scene, and to be sure the theft was recorded, put in the paper, there was the mention of the father's identity. The Moynihan calculation here at work: the facility for dramatic presentation, for playing all the points at once. I can see the pair of us: the little boy sitting on his grandmother's shoulder as she bends forward in her seat and leans on the wooden railing that separates the audience from the council table, see her touch the boy on the leg, urge him to applaud at the right moments in Mayor Smith's inaugural address, her eyes fixed forward and aglow as she waits for the recognition she has set a trap for. She was handsome, capable, accomplished, full of grace, and she wanted to be recognized.

Father, My Father

—for my father, Lewis Hall,
who worked in the Kansas City stockyards

I had to ask and maybe ask again,
but he bought the wool skirt and sweater I wanted.

How often memories are a bath of acid
in which old photographs sat.

My father was a silent man.
His work was his constancy —

his solid footing in the house.
He left and returned each day

with talk of union workers vying for their lives —
who would have power and who wouldn't.

It always got back to that —
the same old song of the world.

I knew the sound of cattle in the stockyards —
the move of their hooves up the wooden ramp

where sparrows sang from the rafters
above the kill floor.

It was as if cattle were given language
in their last cries, telling their stories of the field,

the long discomfort of the travel,
the railroad wheels *clicking clicking* their way to death.

They didn't want to give something,
but they did.

Where the Chips Fall

"This might be worth some money now."
My uncle shows me a tattered black case.
It's unassuming, small, but nestled inside,
six pristine rows of poker chips
stamped with dark brown swastikas
wait for a game. "Found 'em in a dresser
that came with the house."

As my uncle pours a row into my hands,
I see shadowy soldiers flinging chips onto a table;
I smell sweat and cigarette ash,
hear the clatter of chips slapping
against one another. Clack. clack, clack,
like train wheels pulsing on rails,
like shells falling from guns.

Stacks of chips reward the players.
Straight: capture a family from the ghetto,
grandparents, parents, new baby boy.
Three of a kind: beat two pair,
hurl twin brothers to the ground.
Flush: crush five rabbis
wearing black *yarmulkas,*
then stack your winnings into mounds.

Clenching a chip in my fist, I feel
the coolness of its surface,
the heat of the swastika, a snarl of lines.
Six rows of chips, idle for decades,
lying forgotten, their value rising
as the players who used them pass
out of sight. Six rows ready for a new game.

Sheba

In one of the last days of summer,
in a last hour of the day,
when minutes begin to liquefy
and flow to the earth
like thick syrup,
she stood in the doorway
and inhaled
the scent of leaves and grass
drifting through the air,
a tang of death blurring the edges
of the aroma,
fogging the last bits of spice
released by the summer sun.
She lingered in front of the
screened door
listening to cicadas
struggle against their dying,
protesting oblivion.
A turban covered
some sparse strands of her hair,
left after the second round of chemo,
a few curling strands stubbornly clinging
to her scalp like cut roses
cleaving to color and fragrance.
Like Sheba, she looked regal
in her headdress and robe,
straight and strong
to the passerby,
her mind not ready to answer
the question facing
the moth circling the light above her head.

Ancestry as Reality

— for Tarik

it was a friend saying
"look man, divorce
doesn't make bad children,
bad parents do," that stuck
in the weak side of better judgment.
so i pushed against the cycle — poor, black,
    fatherless —
to see if it would break.
it haunts me
with apparitions of my own father
his eyes beady as a pair of craps,
a bottle of cheap gin
on his kitchen table,
him, way off in Omaha.

when the measles, the whooping coughs,
father's day get you, when at school
the skilled surgeons cut the good black stuff
from your head, i may not be there.
but you'll have the weekends, summers,
me pleading — "Tarik, daddy loves you,
do you love daddy?" weekends
when i rub you 'gainst my hairless chest
& try to convince you
i wanted to be a man

American History, Popular Version

George Washington is crossing the Delaware
on a beaten horse.
Alexander Hamilton is dying in a frilly shirt
with a pale woman kneeling over him.
Thomas Jefferson is sitting in dim light
scribbling on a thin parchment.
two men with white wigs are shaking hands
on the porch of a mansion.
Paul Revere's hair is streaming in the wind.
a frail woman is standing at a window.
another is seated at a bureau
brushing her long brown hair.
Abraham Lincoln is walking a dirt road
his big bony wrists sticking from his coat sleeves.

we're down in there somewhere,
a mule with a hard row to hoe,
a pair of black hands
clutching the whitest cotton,
down there grinning
or just seething in silence,
our eyes rolling around in our heads,
our tongues beseeching the burning yellow sun.

Nostalgia of the Mud

—for Etheridge Knight

you remind me of my father—
the pain somehow aesthetic,
the way they've strung you out
over a religion
        that skips Sunday,

turns up red-eyed
'bout 2 o'clock Monday afternoon.

there's a jazz riff, a waywardness
at the core of your Karma,
reminds me of the time
the family was walking from church
& we dug my old man
in the alley drinking wine.

must be we inherit red eyes,
our folk hugged against ghetto walls
bent by so much dark blue living.

give me the bottle too.
hope this poem kills the poison
off the wine we've uncapped
but if not, drink up, pass the grapes 'round.

Allegory of the Bebop Walk

there are uncharted places
like Overland Park, Kansas, or Greenwich, Conn.
where they'd lock the back door
if they heard black power was coming
'cause black folk wouldn't dare
come 'round the front.

in these territories
our faces are long survivors
from days of stingy brims
and pointed shoes, or Rochester, Beaulah and co.,
days of a million changes
until a bebop walk broke down before the logic

of a stiff gait, logic that is visa
into white and light domains.

now there's no way back
and no convenient solace within miles
just a vast unfamiliar turf
and a few of us looking in vain
for Afro-Sheen in the suburban drugstore.

Something Else They Say

is that jazz is dead
but i want to tell you
that in a wooden loft in Chicago
Archie Shepp gave artificial respiration
to a carcass.

no gimmicks,
no electricity coming from his sax,
just the naked instrument
that hung limp
from a thin red tie.

Shepp was dressed in a 1950 cotton suit,
faded and slick like rat fur.
when the sounds got good to him
he took off his coat
and turned to the band.
his hip pocket was snagged from years
of dragging a gin bottle.

as he blew
the words of critics flaked away.
the music they say is dead
was so alive, it sweated.

Emotional Alzheimer's
from "Crazyology: A Kaleidoscope of Carnality"

The speaker is a woman in a coffee shop.

WOMAN

I had lunch with one of my friends last week, and we were talking about our exes, and I said "I'm over him, I really am." And when I said it, I suddenly choked up; and my friend jumps me, "See? You're in denial. You think you're over him but you're not." But see, I *am* over him, and when I said it I choked up not because I'm kidding myself, but because it's true. I realized as I was saying it that if you can lose the person that matters to you most, and after awhile they don't matter at all, then what does that say about us? I've got Emotional Alzheimer's.

My grandmother had real Alzheimer's. My whole life I was always her 'angel,' but there came a time when she didn't know her angel anymore. And for awhile she was still happy because there was this wonderful stranger who'd bring food to *her*, a woman who couldn't remember when she ever had a friend. But then finally there came a time when she didn't remember you have to eat. So when I came with food, the angel she used to love had turned into some terrible person pestering her about pickiunie things.

So when I say I'm over my ex, I mean it. And now I'm over being upset about not being upset.

And it used to be I couldn't talk about my grandmother without choking up. But now I can do that too.

So, who's not going to matter next?

13

from **Never Say Die**

A team of young, minor baseball players are in a cheap locker room, so cheap there are no lockers, just pegs for their clothes. The players listen to Moose Corwin, a former World Series hero who is now their manager.

MOOSE

You know the best feeling in the world?
You walk out on the field on the road and people boo coz you're the best, and they know it, and they're jealous, and they're thinking, "We're gonna knock you off this time, we're gonna bring you down."
Made my adrenaline flow.
When I was with the Yankees my favorite games were the close ones with big rivals at the end of the season on the road. The whole season's on the line, the noise of the crowd getting louder every inning, the tension, the screaming, the hot dog vendors and beer vendors all set their stuff down to watch, and everybody's watching, everybody's screaming, sixty thousand people hoping you screw up, and then their best runner reaches first,
and the whole world knows he'll try to steal second,
and he's waiting and watching, waiting,
and there he goes,
and there's sixty thousand screams,
and you make the throw
and he slides and there's a cloud of dust
and the screams get louder and he's
out!...
And the game's over,
and the season's over,
and you hear sixty thousand groans,
and then. . . silence.
That silence was my. . . personal reward.
You can know that feeling too.

from *"Black Pearl Sings!"*

The speaker is Pearl, an African-American from one of the South Carolina sea islands. She explains to a song collector from the Library of Congress why she left the island, and why she doesn't want to celebrate or talk about voodoo and folk beliefs.

PEARL

My husband — before he was my husband — he come back to the island for his mother's funeral.

People come to the praise house all sick. He ask why so many people sick? Minister say it be the will of God. Too many people not Godly enough. But my husband say, "My mother was a Godly woman. But she get sick and die. You tellin' me God wanted that to happen?" Minister say, "Some people had conjure spirits and spells put on 'em." And my husband look around and say, "You want to know why people dyin'? Look where your church's outhouse is. It's dug too close to the well. It's leaking into your drinkin' water. You want a miracle to make people live? Dig your outhouse farther away."

How you think people take that? The conjure woman, she was feelin' powerful: folks think people dyin' coz of her hoodoo, so she don't like it. The minister, he don't like it coz nobody foolish likes bein' told they's foolish. That night buncha rocks git throwed at Thomas's house. The holy people and the hoodoo people probly bump into each other runnin' away.

Next day Thomas come to my house. He whistle me out. He say, "Pearl, I like you. You a good woman. Why don't you come with me to Texas? Texas will be the Garden of Eden. And then he say he goin' *now*. I got to decide *right then*. And I do. I turn my back on my family and all the foolishness you want to celebrate.

Now do I tell people that every night?

Starting from Ellis Island

My family immigrated to New York
so we could make our choice in life.
Starting from Ellis Island
our name was two syllables shorter;
we learned the word 'shortchanged.'

My mother did part-time work
putting cotton balls in pill bottles;
my father drove an ice truck, smoked cigars
that smelled like old tires burning.
I walked a girl home who wasn't Catholic:
he said I was no better than him, or God,
if I wanted to carry on the business
and drive his ice truck when his days were through,
I'd better let her go…
so I signed up with Uncle Sam,
went to fight in the mountains
not far from where my father was born,
not far from where he feared life on the farm.

Our priest sent me a note hinting
how at my father's deathbed my mother sat
worried how the kids ate at the neighbors,
worried why I sent no letters.
I'd crossed enough burned down farms
it showed in my footsteps.

Coming back, I looked in the hatch
at coffins stacked like blocks of ice;
I thought of my father.
If he'd lived, refrigerators
would have put him out of business.

I climbed the Statue of Liberty to kill time,
looked out at Ellis and thought of my father's farm.

All he could be sure of coming here was a country
he couldn't understand.
From this day on I'll be my father's son.

On the Beach At Night

– for JW

Walking at night alone along the beach,
I hear from a house above the shore
the tinkle of a piano hesitantly playing –
too imperfect to be anything but live –
Bach's "Jesu: Joy of Man's Desiring"
though played with only the right hand;
the melody tentatively tapped out
at the rate of a heartbeat
but audible only between the waves
then swallowed by the ocean's surge and roar,
thoughtless sounds that will grate on
long after music and man are gone;
but a half hour later on my walk back
with thoughts darker than the ocean's black,
what was tentative has turned tender,
ragged melody has become song
so that I'm brought to my knees in the sand
and almost weep, but don't,
until the player adds the left hand.

Write Paris out of the Pictures

Tel Aviv's face wears a makeup
of ash. Dust climbs
cheekbone to eyelash.

In the open face of light
women hide like spiders in a well
(*I am not well, I am not well*).

Here comes the junk man
with his little cart
and horse skeleton.

The apartment floods
with dreams — *how much
for the wedding ring?*

Trade a necklace of bullet shells
while the windows rain.
A suicide of buildings.

The landscape blushes,
redly bruised. Hair
unraveling at the root.

Alleys collect finger bones,
calicos and crying.
A soldier touches my crying,

my sun-freckled breasts.
Drink and the wine
licks our bruised lips.

We cannot go to the movies.
Streets are closed.
We race to where the city

ends. The beach is riddled,
waters bleed. Days
crumble unceremoniously.

Black and White

A woman lets a sheep suckle
her nipple. Anonymous,

her face hidden
by a soiled man's hat.

Stained yellow sweater,
unbuttoned blue dress.

The sheep's face
pressed to her pinkness.

Sheep and breast,
lost lovers.

> (One who gives,
> one who takes.)

Behind them, a burnt field
and dozens of bone-thin legs.

Hungry sheep hunt
for a single blade

while this one drinks
what others will die for.

A woman, another kind
of grass.

Egg and Envy

To be chosen, perceived
singularly

against all those teeth,
millions of miles of want

muttered into the sky.
Desire, an illness:

one breaks,
one wins, twin

born without a twin
(one crushes, and lives).

Every voice, a hiss
with my name inside

and God in the rafters
hissing too. All my life

the chosen one, a lie
the great book told

along with floods,
doves, a plucked rib

and a woman converted
to salt. In Truth,

choking on it,
my clotted mouth,

my face a blanket of skin,
generic, unchosen, storyless.

Somewhere between anonymous
and *hiss, hiss.*

Roughing In

Like Dante's fallen lovers
Paolo and Francesca,
the plumber seeks perpetual union.

Where cast iron's lowered
on shoulders of apprentices,
pitch rubs off
on the right side of their faces —
a procession of one-sided men
toward slope and sump.

Below slightest wind, the plumber
cradles a chalice of hot lead,
the outward sign
of yellow smoke spreading

where spadefuls of wet clay
lie on their backs, the long
Our Father beads of Italian laborers.

Water lapses into a single
way of life,
spiraling into circles
of good works and waste

where the life of this world
cures under concrete —
epistles in vulgate,
the cloistered credo
of disposal and redemption.

Waiting for the Plumber

Things seldom leak
where they drip

a thin layer of water
may disguise itself as chrome
or travel the patterns of wallpaper
into your bed at night

perhaps a flashing has come loose
on the roof,
or war has broken out
on the other side of the world,
transgressions start long before
they come through the wall

just get a pan
till the plumber arrives.

There are women, too, whose lives
seep out
into their children
almost overnight,
yet you cannot find the breaches of love
in their eyes.

This, too, is a plumber's nightmare.

The simplest gestures may baffle
as soon as they leave our hands:
The congressman on his way to prison
says he will wear his conviction
"like a badge of honor."

You know the corrosion
lies far back in the plumbing

where elbows, Ts and Ys
can turn us around, unable
to tell the source from the ends,
where the water itself begins
making false statements.

No Theory

Leave me here in the century
where I was born, the old century
of levers, knobs, vacuum tubes,
furnace stacks, scrubbers, and lead
filling the sky, tons of lead,
through which I sail, like a bird
born with a mysterious cell
in its brain for the route home.
Who walks the hundred years?
Voice commands, retina twitches
turn and return from satellites, now,
without bones or muscles or clear
membranes that protect the eye.
I suppose getting lost no longer
will be possible, or to be helpless
and alone with only a prayer
or raft made of railroad ties,
which wobbles on a wave, like love.
Only now have I gotten the Ford truck
to start in the driveway, its white
cough appearing in the mirror,
hazing the air between my house
and the power pole, a pole stitched
in wires and cables — switches
to those who know but do not talk.
I love to sit in the cab and shudder
with moisture, while air and gasoline

heat up the engine block and radiate
energy into the hole that looks at God.
In the rivers I know, a boy would not
dare stick even a leg — alligator gar
gulping cattle carcasses, fertilizer,
uranium, Styrofoam packages, sulfites,
latex particles, unrecycled refrigerators.
Always we have been weighted down,
and in 1968 I stood at the back door
of Sheehan Plumbing Co. on Delmar
in St. Louis, the morning after the Memphis
shooting, that shooting, with young Joe,
the owner, and his big Irish-green trailer
and lengths of cast-iron and clay pipe,
and half bricks that had set off alarms
all night, piles of glass, copper fittings,
and lead rings — the metal of the century,
which yellowed the shop air when melting,
like gold breathing, and we breathed it.
It's in there, now, in our lungs, foiled
onto each aspiration of the century —
to stamp-press, to mold, caste and cart
the sky, itself, as the morning of my birth,
chalked with pigeon dung on the ledges
and shoulders burnished bronze, where
a white boy would not even be allowed
to get himself so dirty. I did apply
for work in the dung stables, the manholes
shining with the backs of bugs, and once,
my father stood on a chair at a construction site
to order three-hundred men back to work.
They were protesting new faces in the united
nations of the union, not far from the mines
of central Missouri, where blacks had died
as well, my father knew, in the great strike
of '22, and heavy metals flowed with rainbows
and coal into the creeks. You could taste

what was silently offered from the ground,
the ground from which we pulled this lead.
I think I can still name my friends dead
of mortar fire, half a world and other century
away. They are lying low and fixed
in stone, barely able even now to keep quiet.

The Narrow Gate

"Holy Land," Ellen Pearce's cover painting for a 2010 edition of *New Letters*, draws viewers to its blasts of color and light. "Beautiful," I often hear; then the viewer realizes, "Those are bombs. That's blood down there." If art demands transcendence, it does so through the visible, the actual, and allows us time to see beyond. Not for no reason does Pearce's painting include a non-natural opening of light, a rectangle, like a door or window, something human-made we might call an alternate choice. The artist, there, gives us a "narrow gate" to go through—as the gospel of Matthew advises in Willis Barnstone's *Restored New Testament*—among the wide-ranging and nearly organic images of war. I see the squared-off shape that way because I choose to, and because I can. The artist leaves the choice, finally, to me.

Art seeks that magical brightness, which is not often easy, not often expedient. I write this on the Feast of All Saints, which would seem the height of convention, even comfort, among church goers. Not so. The saints won't let it happen. Take "saints" here in the larger, unofficial view—as Emerson wrote, "When the half-gods go,/ The gods arrive." This morning, I heard a Jesuit priest celebrate an Austrian farmer by the name of Franz Jägerstätter, a husband with three daughters, and the only Roman Catholic in his town, in the early 1940s, to declare himself anti-Nazi. When Jägerstätter asked Church authorities to explain the contradiction between Church teaching and the Church's own acquiescence to Hitler's policies, they couldn't. They said what others in their position have said over the years: They were following orders. Those orders formed the wide landscape of that time and place. In 1943, Jägerstätter refused service in Hitler's army and chose, instead, to go through the narrow gate — into prison, in his case, where the forces of Third Reich cut off his head.

The story dramatizes something more important even than heroism. It alerts us to the ease with which we, as a culture, can come to accept the wide landscape as normal and acceptable. I often have wondered how I would have responded to certain historical events, and I have no confidence that I would have done the right or the brave thing. I am encouraged, however, by the fortitude of others, such as writer and activist Edward Sanders, in an interview in the same *New Letters* issue, shown to be practicing his convictions at the age of 70. One can read poems, stories, and essays by people confronting different kinds of ideologies, cultural or otherwise, inflicted upon them and others — like military vet Roy Scranton, pondering his left-over military gear: "I want to keep everything. I want to throw it all away." Or Renée Giovarelli, an American woman working on aid projects in Kyrgyzstan, unwilling to be intimidated by a male deputy minister with a big hat. These stories, poems, and essays show people in various stages of doubt and trepidation; the stories are personal and political and cultural; and every one required conviction to write.

"To believe fully and at the same time to have doubts is not at all a contradiction," writes philosopher Rollo May in *The Courage to Create*. "It presupposes a greater respect for truth, an awareness that truth always goes beyond anything that can be said or done at any given moment." Rollo May understands the dual nature of art, especially literary art, in which a reader or character comes into conflict with a prevailing force, external or internal; and someone, reader or character, will be called to make a choice. What could be more exciting, or important?

Franz Jägerstätter has been beatified by the Church but not yet canonized. Here's the good news. He already has taken his stand, which is all that matters. More good news: Ellen Pearce does not say what she intended by that rectangle of light in her painting, "Holy Land." Maybe she expects us to step through.

What a Poem Can Teach Us
from *On Swerving: The Way of William Stafford*

The Tao teaches us humility as we seek our place in the order and harmony of the cosmos. There is a relationship established here. To go with "the way," the Tao, has been termed in Chinese as *wu wei*, sometimes translated "actionless activity." Neither active nor inactive. This is the eternal principle of seeking oneness with all that exists. "Like any other sustained human endeavor," William Stafford once said, "writing is best done in a condition of humility and welcoming of what comes."

We know that William Stafford had firm beliefs. He rejected "action" in World War II by accepting action as a conscientious objector. He spent 1942 to 1946 in work camps in Arkansas, California, and Illinois and was paid $2.50 per month to fight fires, plant trees, and build roads. In 1944 while in California, he met and married Dorothy Frantz, the daughter of a minister of the Church of the Brethren. Despite all those things, we aren't to get his values confused with what his poems can teach us. "The other source of my unrest," he once told an interviewer, "is that the whole validity of poetry is based on something other than just the shoveling in of content: poetry is an experience."

As a writer, a poet, myself, I approach the work of artists such as William Stafford almost as if I were a highway robber, a bandit, rummaging around in the pockets of what they have to say for inspiration and ideas I can use. *Give it to me*, I think. I am looking for something to sustain me. So, I look into his poem "Remembering Brother Bob," from *A Glass Face in the Rain*, 1982, and I ask what example this poem sets for me.

The speaker of the poem, age twelve at the time, had brought his brother, seven, to a frozen pond to play hockey, and the poem sets off by asking us to look at what actually happened, to look at what is present:

> The sun went down. I turned
> and Bob was crying on the shore.

The center strophe, which follows those lines, pushes the stakes and says, like Socrates, that the unexamined life is not worth living.

> Do I remember kindness? Did I
> shield my brother, comfort him?

This poem sets the example for me of healthy uncertainty, self-examination, which leads to the acceptance of responsibility:

> Yes, I carried him. I took
> him home. But I complained. . . .
>
> "You said you would be brave," I chided
> him. "I'll not take you again."

William Stafford, as a teacher, followed a principle he called "no praise, no blame," in which all issues are in the particulars. Like the scientist Roald Hoffmann, we could say that misjudgments, moments of weakness, bursts of anger, all become part of a process that allows us to seek equilibrium. Stafford ends this poem by returning to observed fact—he chided his brother, "I'll not take you again" — but this time, the facts carry more weight. No praise, no blame. The speaker is neither victim nor villain, but someone who accepts fully the range of his actions.

> Years, I look at the white across
> this page and think: I never did.

I remember the first time I met William Stafford in person, back in the late 1970s, when he read his poems in Kansas City. He probably was sixty-four or sixty-five years old at the time, and after he finished reading, a girl about ten years old raised her hand. "Mr. Stafford," she said, "when did you become a poet?"

His reply is one of the things that has sustained me many times over the years whenever I find the need to examine my own life as a writer. In retrospect, the more I learned about the man, the more his statement seemed to fit him. "Whenever anyone asks that," he said, "I always like to turn the question around and ask the adults in the room: 'When did you stop being a poet?'"

28

Is There Time to Compose?

1.

I feel an old man in me,
Suffering from amnesia.
He is afraid there is not enough time
To learn to love you.

2.

You remind me tonight of the beautiful
Ancient stringed instrument I once saw.
Your body's sweet music confuses my desire.
Shall I risk irreverence? —
Putting my clumsy, shivering fingers to
Those delicate strings.
Or try to push closed that cold iron door —
Hoping no one else hears your luring melody?
But your eyes make me bold,
And I will strengthen my armour —
Hoping that Beethoven did not compose
The last great symphony.

Looking Ahead

Why while watering the seed
Do I climb the tree?
Inside it is beautiful —
So I climbed the tree today.
I longed to see the forbidden future,
To know if you and I held each other
Somewhere past that horizon.
But friend, it is only within you.
She does not want to know.
The meadow around that tree —
Can it be so small?
"Through her eyes you could not even see it.
No leaves have turned green in her."
Why should they?
I am the unfortunate lover.
I want to see ten sunsets tonight in one sky.

Late Words

Late words
may not be the
best words
but they are the
last words
one would have thought of
uttering

First words
bespeak riddle words but
late words
say everything or
nothing

Before the Eclipse

My husband calls me
to the window
the night before the eclipse.
Jupiter is rising
toward the full moon.

My thoughts rise
with this brightest star
then fall, thinking of our son
who has signed up
for the army.

The recruiter calls.
Our son can enter earlier.
"I can get him in by the end
of this month," he says.

I hang up the phone
and wonder if I should pass
the message to this boy
who wants to be a man,
this boy who wants to prove himself,
this boy who wants to belong.

He sits in the cool quiet
of the bright night
fishing from a borrowed kayak
a million miles from the moon
and the war
watching Jupiter rising
toward the full moon
the night before the eclipse.

My 90-Year-Old Father and My Husband Discuss Their Trips to the Moon

—for Bill

On the balcony I hear my father
speak of craters, their depth, their breadth;
how he measured his lunar steps so as not to falter,

sidestepping their cavernous mouths to peer in,
his echo resounding in their hearts.
He was on the moon's good side, the one

that smiles and on occasion winks at earth.
With audible pride, he explains he was the lone
civilian on the mission. Yet he was happy to come home.

Yes, my husband says, *it was wonderful for me, too!*
Shepard led me by the hand around the rim
of Erathosthenes. My father laughs at the similarity

of the crater's name to his own, Erasmus.
He is glad Bill understands him,
relieved someone else knows how desolate it can be

out there. *Not only desolate,* Bill says,
putting an arm around my father's frail shoulders,
I also know how lonely it can get.

The Fall

And yet another ode to fall and falling,
another tribute to October light,
to bushes burning in defiance of night,
to Monet, Seurat. Ah, but not until

you've seen an Ozark autumn, not until
then can you understand the plight of Eve,
can you fathom passion, blasphemy.
Apples red, ready, *blur* beside the sensuous

leaf about to fall.
                    Yes, she must have sensed
the beauty of the consequence — else why
bite into shame? The promise of gold obscures
all reason, good intentions, God — luring

us into the daze of earthly glitter,
into the pyre (is that then what it's all
about — gold and ashes?) into blazing
in a moment of orgasmic fury —

and *dying* —
            if only to create fire.

Flag Day at Union Cemetery

—for Tim Barnhart

I enter the clearing
the way we sometimes enter dreams,
the door to the afternoon
clicking behind me,
caution setting like a sun.

On my own, I stand in the center
of this hard-edged lawn,
dwarfed and domed
by a neutered sky, and wonder
how long it would take to turn
me into stone, dust, song—
a process rousing itself
with every incarnation.

When we were children, we'd
whirl each other around,
our skirts unfurling
like these 5,000 banners
waving from the dead—
then we'd let go

and each spun form
would freeze at a command,
breath and laughter chiseled
into pillars, like the headstones here—
exclamations marking
each life's absurd spin, guffawing
in perfect unison,
in perfect deadly rows.

new shoes and an old flame

shopping today i see a pair of kinky
yves st. laurent
shoes and
think of you
now why do you
suppose my mind
not unlike bubble
 gum pushed to its
  very limits springs
   back upon your image
    sticking to the thought
     of you wondering how
      you'd feel about those
       skinny call-girl heels cause
        i'm still   coming on to you
         you see   even though i
         tell my-   self you're gone
         now one   of those people we
         speak   of with reverence or a
         hint of   smile suggesting something
         deeper   than we ever let on   your name
         s t i l l   makes me smile and think of
         high-   heel shoes—the higher, the better

The Blue Booby

The blue booby lives
on the bare rocks
of Galápagos
and fears nothing.
It is a simple life:
they live on fish,
and there are few predators.
Also, the males do not
make fools of themselves
chasing after the young
ladies. Rather,
they gather the blue
objects of the world
and construct from them

a nest—an occasional
Gaulois package,
a string of beads,
a piece of cloth from
a sailor's suit. This
replaces the need for
dazzling plumage;
in fact, in the past
fifty million years
the male has grown
considerably duller,
nor can he sing well.
The female, though,

asks little of him—
the blue satisfies her
completely, has
a magical effect

on her. When she returns
from her day of
gossip and shopping,
she sees he has found her
a new shred of blue foil:
for this she rewards him
with her dark body,
the stars turn slowly
in the blue foil beside them
like the eyes of a mild savior.

The Lost Pilot

—for my father, 1922 – 1944

Your face did not rot
like the others — the co-pilot,
for example, I saw him

yesterday. His face is corn-
mush: his wife and daughter,
the poor ignorant people, stare

as if he will compose soon.
He was more wronged than Job.
But your face did not rot

like the others — it grew dark,
and hard like ebony;
the features progressed in their

distinction. If I could cajole
you to come back for an evening,
down from your compulsive

orbiting, I would touch you,
read your face as Dallas,
your hoodlum gunner, now,

with the blistered eyes, reads
his braille editions. I would
touch your face as a disinterested

scholar touches an original page.
However frightening, I would
discover you, and I would not

turn you in; I would not make
you face your wife, or Dallas,
or the co-pilot, Jim. You

could return to your crazy
orbiting, and I would not try
to fully understand what

it means to you. All I know
is this: when I see you,
as I have seen you at least

once every year of my life,
spin across the wilds of the sky
like a tiny, African god,

I feel dead. I feel as if I were
the residue of a stranger's life,
that I should pursue you.

My head cocked toward the sky,
I cannot get off the ground,
and, you, passing over again,

fast, perfect, and unwilling
to tell me that you are doing
well, or that it was a mistake

that placed you in that world,
and me in this; or that misfortune
placed these worlds in us.

Coda

Love is not worth so much;
I regret everything.
Now on our backs
in Fayetteville, Arkansas,
the stars are falling
into our cracked eyes.

With my good arm
I reach for the sky,
and let the air out of the moon.
It goes whizzing off
to shrivel and sink
in the ocean.

You cannot weep;
I cannot do anything
that once held an ounce
of meaning for us.
I cover you
with pine needles.

When morning comes,
I will build a cathedral
around our bodies.
And the crickets,

who sing with their knees,
will come there
in the night to be sad,
when they can sing no more.

Graveside

Rodina Feldervatova,
the community's black angel —
well, we come to you,

having failed to sink
our own webbed fingers
in the chilled earth where

you hang out. I think
you are doomed to become
symbols for us that we

will never call by name.
But what rifles through
our heads is silence, one

either beyond or below
whatever it is that we do
know. We know by heart,

don't we? We've never
learned. And we bring what
we have known to you, now,

tonight. Open your home
to us, Rodina. Kiss
our brains. Tell us that

we are not drunk, and
that we may spend
our summers with you.

Up Here

The motel was made for love
as you were. I undressed you
with grace and tenderness,
kissing each newly bared part.

There you lay, your small, white
body throbbing in my hand
like a bird. We were silent.
The right word was not needed.

Supple. What was I doing
suddenly pacing around
the bed, scratching my head,
staring down at your gaze up
at me? *Recognition.*

I would not call you *svelte.*
Your breasts were barely a hand-
ful; I like small breasts, which fit
a hand. Your thighs were a feast,
though, and, walking, now and then
I would dip down to nibble
them. They were good: *wholesome.*
They were the bread of life.

Now your lips are moving, now
your hands reach up at me.
I feel as if I might be one
or two thousand feet above you.

Your lips form something, a bubble,
which rises and rises into
my hand: inside it is a word:
Help. I would like to help,
believe me, but up here nothing
is possible, nothing is clear:
Help. Help me.

Facts of Life

My father, teetotaler, vegetarian,
took two baths a day,
one at dawn the other
before his evening obeisance
to lord Shiva at the temple.

Cleanliness of forms,
the given and the gifted,
adherence to principles,
honesty, truth, purity,
were things he'd die for.

Yet he died of a malignancy
whose virtue was pillage,
whose form spread
from viscera to vision,
from body to soul.

Now he who loved roses
lies buried within limits
of his caste's cemetery
by the river Kabini
where the banyans sway,

where transients and pilgrims
come to celebrate Shiva's victory
over one demon or another.

Mount Pleasant, USA

at night
I'm a man surprising himself
in sleep a slight stirring of the curtains
    at the window the flies kiss
                the bottles to their heart's content
        the glass
is stiff with their chanting

        each night I shift
    to another place
    to another failure
in Iowa I dream of Nanjangud
        my mother
the illiterate waiting
her eyes gone dim her hair
                off to nowhere ...

given up on sons given up on herself
waiting the night for the day
to be over for the day to begin

        in the bars
of Chicago in the scowl
of Mount Pleasanteans in the handshake
of friends in the flashback
of promises in my exile

the cage I carry is the cage I made

Stillness

the hours
sullen goats grazing on emptiness
drift mutely to the other side of day

the sun has cast his mid-day net
but doesn't move
to pull in the catch —

a chameleon
two stink bugs stiff after love
a towhee dozing over my patch of impatiens

stillness is making its point
knowing this
the wind plays dead

Poets in Groups

In their photographs,
they stand frozen to permanence.
Only the eyes,
in that fraction of second
when they squint
reveal their fears,
hushed, slanted,
paddled deep into a swirl.

You sense
the birds in their thoughts
sullen on branches sagging with snow,
the monkish light pacing beyond black boughs,
the familiar echoes
in the dream valley,
a boat fishtailing into mist.

How much is hidden and why
is only assumed
like the line
in the subconscious,
their faces, made blank, do not show the depths

in which they're held.

A Brief Discussion
of Heisenberg's Uncertainty Principle

> ... *the very act of observing disturbs a system, introducing*
> *a certain percentage of uncertainty allowing for extreme*
> *changes in motion or position.*

To the rest of us kids,
my sister brought the news of the birth.
Ten tiny beings pushed from *the bowels*
of her hamster.
I was the first to her bedroom door.
She'd moved the male to another cage
where he ran off his irritation
on a squeaky wheel.
I watched the shiny, electric pink things
emerge from torn tissue paper
and disappear within the scraps again,
moving in miniscule increments.
The female cleaned them,
licked their translucent bodies.
I had to imagine them breathing.
When I leaned against the bedroom's doorframe.
its flimsy wood creaked
and the wheel went silent.
The female's brown head pivoted,
and the onyx beads of her eyes
were a starless night sky.
Then she began to eat her babies.
From the ether of tissue scraps,
she gathered each with quick claws,
bit through them, *pop, snick;*
her bloody teeth carved them, reduced them;
her paws stuffed them into her mouth,
all before my brother and my sister

arrived beside me.
She ate them as I watched —
as their position in time and space
changed forever.
That night, lying in bed
I stared into the absolute dark
and thought how we'd all want to speak to God
but never want to see
his impossibly white,
shining teeth.

How a Bird is Born

The small one,
the one we carried to the tree,
the one we carried to the river,
the one we carried to the mountain,
and then up through the clatter of rocks,
up past the caves' moaning holes,
up to the tiny table of the peak,
and then to the moist sky.
The sky that draped
our shoulders in shawls of mist,
the sky that granted
only enough air to dance
under the cold sun.
We offered it up
to the darkness
that crouches at the edge
of the blue wind.
The small one,
the one joined with the sky,
the one we carried,
the one we sang
into the blue, into the black,

the black that feeds the stars
and grants the wings
made from all the light.

The Sea is the Longest Breath

– for Crystal

The sea is the longest breath ever taken.
Its vast green chest rises again
before it can completely fall –
forever pumped by wind and moon.
This sailboat's engine is like
the biggest heart that ever beat,
its rhythm so strong the bulkheads hum.
Between this heart and that breath
a song drifts out over the sea.
It is the longest song ever sung.
It goes on for days,
passed on from hull to waves,
as we plunge and heave and roll
across the sea's nervous chest.
This song is for you.
Now you are the sea, the wind,
the moon and the song
that rises up to sting my eyes,
to coat my hair in salt.
Sing on past the time
the boat rests sluggish in its slip,
on softly to my ears at night
when I am alone,
into my dreams where we both
stand on deck before I awaken
and you turn to me to say,
the sea is the longest breath ever taken.

Solutions

*Many solutions, of varying strengths, are required in a good
chemistry lab.* —Chemistry text, 1964

My father gave me his glass bottles.
In them I mixed my buffer, molar and normal solutions.
For them he built a shelf
that hung from the ceiling in my basement lab,
his offering to my education.
The fifths, quarts, pints and half-pints
ranged across the shelf in orderly rows
labeled for my tests and experiments.
Each bottle, my uniform history of learning,
was an example of my calculations:
grams, milliliters, atomic weights.
Throughout the week I found gleaming bottles,
washed out, labels removed, waiting
like gifts on my lab counter,
or on the floor by his bed.
For each I prepared a new solution.
One day hid shouts and curses, his feet stomping
to the door above my head dissolved my experiment.
Down the stairs he announced he was going
to shoot my mother and that bastard
she ran with at the dance studio.
I calculated it just right, up and out in time
to jump into the car as he backed away.
It was just he and me and the big Smith and Wesson
on the seat between us.
He parked down the street like a cheap detective
and stared at the studio's entrance
with such concentration that not a soul
went in or came out, until dusk filled our eyes.
He pulled himself from the car, leaned against the door.
I emptied the revolver because I knew
the atomic weight of lead that filled my hand.

He asked for the gun, reaching inside.
Standing in the night air, the gun
stretching his arm, he looked in at me.
I pointed toward the red sign two blocks down.
So he gave in,
and we bought another useful bottle.

The Farmer's Widow at His Grave

Rest now and let your knuckles grow smooth.
Hammer no clouds against the sky.
On this hillside, conjure no more grain.
Let fences and sheds fall down.
Let the combines rust.
Let all things be as they will be.
Let our youthful design complete itself
as the landscape subscribes,
by sun, vermin and the wind's fury.
No longer will I come into this field
with food and drink and a lover's kiss.
No longer will we bloody our hands
at the rush of a newborn calf.
No longer will we sleep with the sunset
or dress together at first light.
Forget these things and the sayings of men.
They explain nothing
of the formations of your face,
tilled by seasons of infidelities,
nothing of your stooped shape, your knuckles
busted and scabbed by frozen mornings,
nothing of the hues of the afternoons
that stretched our shadows
beyond all reckoning.

Pear Season

If I buy you a new dress,
a short one in a floral pattern
cut deep from the shoulders,
and a wide-brimmed straw hat,
will you stand beneath the trees
before the pears fall and rot,
barefoot, hair tumbling from chapeau,
wearing only that dress
and nothing more,
and lift the hem high enough
to show the place where your thighs
meet the roundness of your cheeks?
Fill the dress then with ample pears
so I can make for you
French butter pears in raspberry sauce
to go with a glass of red wine
this evening on the wooden deck
as the colors of the treetops change
and before we go back inside
to escape the coming chill.
I promise not to photograph you
or tell anyone what we've done.
I'll just remember you one autumn afternoon
when we couldn't hold enough of each other,
when the pears were so many
there wasn't time between us
to gather them all.

Breaking the Drought

Three inches of rain! On the Kansas prairie,
those drowning in dust open their throats.
Listless milo, stunted corn, ragweed

and wild alfalfa stand tall. Only the Western
spruce, backyard survivor of endless high winds,
branches burned brown by waterless skies,

shows no change. Its owner, at ninety twice the age
of her tree, tough as buffalo grass, fragile as winter
wheat at harvest, jokes, "Everything is half dead

and half alive, including me." We call for an expert.
The County Agent pokes and pinches, breaks off
brittle twigs, notes how few nodes the tree produced

for spring growth. When he delivers the news—
we could wait and see how it does through winter,
hope for revival—I'm tempted to agree. But when

my mother says, "Let's cut it down," I understand:
finally, something she can relieve of its suffering,
something that can come to a clear and certain end.

Summer

Suspended by one strand of spiderweb, seedburst
hovers and swings, counting out time, scribbling its sign
that this world is cursed with repletion, blessed with waste.
One wind shift, and light gray fence rails darken with rain.
God gets to *assign* meaning to the three gray cats
crouched at an open door looking out through the screen,
to round rocks clattering, to the fly that insists
on entreating my right arm again and again.
Even dry months host a luxury of moonlight,
a sybaresis of dry leaves, of sprinkler spray
blown onto a neighbor's yard, of last plums picked at
by thirsty birds, paving stones tree roots lift and splay,
holes eaten into leaves at even intervals and straight,
sons following fathers, swinging their arms the same way.

Fall

Rusting bulldozer, rusting wellhead and backhoe,
rusting LTD. One last hummingbird, rust-necked,
trusts red among rusting cannas. Through the window,
a voice calling *Come on back, that's it, come on back,*
a swingset's rusty voice severed by a chainsaw,
then, thinned by the mile from the road to here, a truck
gearing down. Just briefly, a cluster of sparrows
musters on the screen, each bird clinging, feet and beak,
caught between the mute inward spiral and the one
that speaks, between those dead leaves that as they fall
tap the dying to follow and the yellow-brown
dying that argue among themselves how to call
the dead back, between the pepper blushing top-down
and the buddleia's brown base erasing purple.

To Appreciate a Garden

To appreciate a garden, be a worm, the soil rich, loose, and you so valued. Each time the soil is turned, you — fat, squiggling back to your garden life — are celebrated. You eat your way through earth, tunneling through roots, the beauty above you made possible by your dark satisfactions.

To appreciate a garden, be an ant. Crawl over the tight buds of peonies and keep that legend alive, even though they do not need you to open. Find the strawberries, before birds and gardeners, and crawl right into that sweetness. Climb the okra toward that sweet opening of purple and cream flower — hurry, it will only be there for one day. March toward what you know to be sticky, creamy, ambrosial.

To appreciate a garden, be a bee, for everything flowers sweetly before it fruits and seeds, each to its season. Roses love you, as do elderberry, blueberry, hawthorn, thyme and sage. Lavender and sedum compete for your attention, while clematis climbs higher and higher on impossible trellises. That's okay — you can fly.

To appreciate a garden, be a bird. Worm and bee feed you, as do the larvae of cabbage moth, hiding under those broad leaves. Or the swallowtail caterpillar clinging to the lacy edges of fennel. If you are patient, you wait for the strawberries to soften, the bright red cherries to darken, the crab apples to pucker, the mulberries to turn black. You will feast, ignoring scarecrow and pinwheel, flitting through paradise.

To appreciate a garden, be a cat, lying in the shade of okra, Brussels sprouts, green bean and corn. Your master will pat you, glad that your presence keeps squirrels from tomatoes, birds from berries, mice from corn and wheat. After a long morning you might yawn, roll over in the dust and stretch, walk toward water and a small plate of sardines.

To appreciate a garden, be a child. Among vegetables, pick only to eat: cherry tomatoes bursting in your mouth, tender crescent green beans warm and sweet. And who says you don't like salad, at least when served in the garden: the musky celery taste of cilantro, the peppery arugula, the sturdy oak leaf lettuce, the wispy licorice of fennel. Don't stop. There are clusters of broccoli, cucumbers no bigger than your fingers, onion tops to sour in your mouth. Arrive at the watermelon patch and split one open, juice running down your hands, then your chin. You have found your dessert.

To appreciate a garden, be a gardener. From the seeded earth you have brought forth beauty, nutrition, and pleasure enough to last beyond seasons.

To appreciate a garden, be a statue, planted among all that flowers and dies. You will be in the garden through seasons, years, maybe even lifetimes. You are inert, your presence your life.

Éléphants Nageurs

The camera man shoots up
at the feet of elephants
swimming by. On their faces
joy and surprise that the burden
of gravity has been lifted.
Their trunks curl upward
snorkeling air and waving
hallelujah like a gospel choir.
The program is in French,
but no translation is needed.
Nor could any language
explain why they'd obey
the command to come ashore.

Natural Order

The kitchen happens to be
    in the way. Each May the ants

        make their peony pilgrimage,
           follow their doctrine of pheromones

                up cabinets, over counters, down.
                  Dotted lines of monks pepper

the floor. On and on they come
    in a scene from Cecil B. DeMille,

        proceeding as directed.
           Never mind the brief frenzy

                at the cat food bowl. In a miracle
                  of efficiency, they're soon gone.

So I wonder why, for the past
    three nights, a single ant has

        tickled my arm as I sit in
           the next room.   Are there always

                a few lost, unworthy of reaching
                  paradise — the weak, the doubting,

the unrepentant? Or perhaps the same
    ant keeps returning, praying

        I will again blow him aloft,
           longing for the rapture of flight.

from *The Inland Ground:*
An Evocation of the American Middle West

My Middle West, which this book [*The Inland Ground*] is more or less about, with some important omissions and some wanderings off over the hill, was Kansas City, Missouri, and Independence, Missouri. It is a country lake in Kansas as I write. During the years of World War II, we—my widowed father, my brother, and I—moved all over the east side of Kansas City, a lower-middle-class area which is now part of the city's black ghetto, living in boardinghouses and occasionally a real home. I was cared for by German immigrants who believed in education, hard widows who knew how to bread a meat loaf, middle-class mothers in need of extra income, and spinsters heavy with love. If anyone raised me, my older brother did. We lived in the streets, flattening bottle caps on streetcar tracks, walking the high parapets of outdoor billboards, occupying vacant lots, wandering the huge storm sewers that drain Kansas City's rainwater into the Missouri River. We saw *Lassie Come Home* at the National Theater on Independence Avenue and cried, and later saw *Frankenstein* there at night and hardly dared the shadowed walk home. Old Mr. Gernhardt, a German POW from World War I who stayed to become an American citizen, told us of helping to build the Al-Can Highway and sang "Mademoiselle from Armentières" at the piano until Mrs. Gernhardt stopped him.

Unable to find a school library book in my fourth-grade year, I stole a five-dollar bill from my father, bought a box of kitchen matches and a package of notebook paper at the corner drugstore and rode by bus and trolley on a school morning in the wintertime to Swope Park, determined to become a wise and much-consulted hermit there. Climbed the wooded hill to a clearing behind the bronze statue of Colonel Swope, wadded up the notepaper, and lit it. Found no warmth but some wisdom, retraced my path back to school and accepted the principal's mild scolding and my father's amusement. He paid for the book.

We tended no Victory Garden, being renters only, but collected grease and flattened tin cans to help the war effort. The Manor bread man drove through the neighborhood three times a week in a truck pulled by a horse and gave us—a gang of children long ago dispersed and their names forgotten—day-old sweet rolls. And though my brother and I were lonely, those days seem now some paradise for the city and for me. The war occupied adult attentions and eliminated distracting luxuries: with little gasoline available to automobiles, the streets were ours, and a glorious afternoon in midsummer might be magic as simple as a hike up the hill to the Velvet Freeze ice-cream parlor for a butterscotch sundae.

Later, my father remarried, and all our lives for a time became painful. Still the city spared us. Told to leave the house in the morning and not return until night, we biked to the eight-foot trailer of an old woman who lived in a vacant lot beside a creek. She had a cigarette-making machine, and would roll cigarettes for us along with her own. Once she baked a moist, raisiny cake on her hot plate which the three of us ate at one sitting. In her prime she roamed the backroads in her trailer taking portrait photographs of country people. Now she was old, and lived on the little money her son could send her.

And other distractions: school friends; long bike tours to green city parks; watching the doughnut-making machine at the Katz drugstore; reading at the library; selling Christmas cards door to door to earn a chemistry set; swimming at the city pool.

And abruptly, when I was twelve and my brother fourteen, in the summer of 1949, we were removed to the country, to a boys' home run under a private trust, the Andrew Drumm Institute in Independence, Missouri, and found ourselves farmers. Neither of us took easily to farming, having lived in the city as urban Huckleberry Finns, but we had no choice, and so we learned that work, never with the inborn sense of routine that a child raised on a farm possesses, but with some fair imitation of it.

Began cleaning chicken roosts for chores, leading the old mare in and out of the barn to raise and lower the hay hook, straightening whole kegs of nails salvaged from a razed shed, hoeing the forty-acre garden, picking strawberries, planting potatoes, filling up, when the train bell atop the smokehouse called us to supper, on heavy country food. Learning, later, to plow and disk and mow; to feed cattle and clean the barn; to cook for forty people and clean the dormitories; to cut down trees; to weld; to speak in public and conduct a parliamentary meeting; to operate a mangle and a steam press; to drive a school bus and a farm truck; to show a steer and a sheep; to butcher cattle and hogs and chickens; to can tomatoes and cut meat; to paint fences and build a barn; to call hogs and terrace a field; to deliver calves; to dock lambs; to put up silage in the sweet sweaty silo and grind corn in the violent hammer mill. Learning besides to play football and baseball and basketball; to run track; learning plane geometry and algebra and world history; learning vocational agriculture: the anatomy of farm animals, their diseases, their breeding, seeds, crops, fertilizers, woodwork, metalwork, electricity, plumbing, engines, farm machinery.

Feeling at times, in the isolation of adolescence, despair of my past and despair of my future, but never able to sustain such despair for long because the land and the animals and the work always called me back to those things that must be done next, to those daily regularities that insist on the continuation and preservation of the world. Cows must be milked, and animals fed, and these are certainties on which even loneliness must found an alleviation.

Villanelle for the Road

The true way may be found, but at a cost.
The dashboard deity presides and judges.
Recalculating really means *You're lost.*

Is this a bridge that I've already crossed?
I wonder as the snake of traffic nudges
between the tollbooths. What's it going to cost?

I have my doubts, refusing to be bossed
by bland advice a nagging voice begrudges,
recalculating how you got so lost.

This muse would never suit you, Mr. Frost.
Bear left. Turn right. Take ramp. She never fudges.
The road not taken clearly has a cost.

But I'm footloose again, my baggage tossed
behind me. Good-bye, all you drudges!
Recalculating, nothing to be lost,

I roll along the road, a stone unmossed,
a stubborn certainty that never budges,
finding my way regardless of the cost,
recalculating, yes, but never lost.

Quantum Leap

Thanks, Steve Jobs, for
the best last words ever

Physics says that life perhaps
is but a quantum wave collapse,
and what we see as you and I
is merely photons flitting by.

I only know I'm losing traces
left by names and dates and faces.
Soon enough this flesh of mine
will resurrect in form divine.

I will escape from time and grave,
collapsing with a final wave,
and, leaping from the ledge of now,
exclaim *oh wow...oh wow...oh wow.*

Handling the Evidence

Returning from lunch at the Myron Green Cafeteria
we of the jury, heavy with overcooked carrots
and homemade gravy, settle into the box
for the afternoon. A denim jacket gets handed
around. I study the shoulders of the accused
that shaped its slouch. Here is the evidence
(his old pants with the plaster dust lodged in the cuffs)
that he did unlawfully enter. This pair
of ravaged sneakers did, I'm sure, unlawfully
enter. I think of the man being crudely stripped
of these clothes. Handling the evidence of his life
as though I were picking up after a child
half in anger, half in love
I pass it on.

The Boat Builder

He bows over the board to hone the line
from stem to stern along a subtle curve
that instinct and intelligence define.

With equal parts exactitude and nerve,
and love's perfection lofted in his soul,
he coaxes perfect from imperfect tools

in order to achieve a simple goal:
to sail beyond the reach of any rules
but those of wind and water. Cedar curls

in fragrant piles of flotsam at his feet,
while in his mind, a silken wing unfurls,
all plans fulfilled, all purposes complete.

Mahler and Me

Listening to Mahler
I hear the summer's rolling
thunder. My old man
used to say thunder was
angels bowling.
Mahler was a great composer
and I wouldn't mind having
him on my bowling team.
Ball at eye level he would
knock down the piccolos
with their chirps of cheer,
next the flutes and their
high-pitched reverie.
Down go the violins,
so spicy sweet.
Tall stand the bassoons
and oboes of woe.
Bass fiddles, French horns,
keep the ball rolling
with the dirge of shallow
thunder. The lane echoes
the maple tree's heart,
somber notes cling
to the sadness
of the chilling winds.
The cymbals come crashing
as lightning startles the air.
At last the tiny triangle
pings of salvation. And now
comes the rain, harsh.

To Be

Tryouts for the school play:
Miss Castle finally chose me and
three other talented preteen boys
to be elm trees.
Stand tall, raise your arms,
and sway back and forth.
I was the shortest elm tree in Ohio.
My dreams of football, white knighthood,
and a Fonz-like attraction to girls
faded in the quiet shade of the
elm's ego-sapping umbrella.
My sister, a real actor, who wore
makeup and talked to the last row,
said with passion: *BE the tree!*
Your skin will turn to bark, your sway
will match the rhythm of the winds.
You welcome birds and bees.
You ARE an elm.

Opening night we found anxiety
running high. The backdrop dropped,
the speakers sputtered,
and I fought the dark night against
an inexplicable desire to flip into
my soft maple tree mode.
Struggling against the *bête noire*
I prayed for the power
to be me: *Ulmus americana.*
After the performance we
took our bows, the house packed
with seventeen Italian relatives
would not stop clapping till
I came forward to genuflect.
The sap ran sweet
through my fevered boughs.

Taboo

Back then nobody had tattoos
except sailors and drunks.
I was both. Blessed by the sea
and battered by rum.
You will get no apologies from me.
I kept the main sail on course,
I did my job. My word was true,
and I kept the wind out of my mouth.
A taciturn man, they said, without
a sextant to my brain or
a compass to my heart.
Tattoos are popular now.
Tramp stamp, trailer trash, muscle beach,
under the wing, heartfelt, and ginger snake.
Take me home banana boat.
My tattoo is an anchor on my chest
that has sunk to the bottom of the sea.
Time for a new tattoo, a new irrevocable contract
more sure than marriage, less sure than death.
Who can forget his mom, his first love,
the rose, the viper and the twist of permanence?
Not I, sir, they are always with me.
For myself, I will take a single unguarded
musical note to sing my song.
I will place it on the back of my wrinkled hand
and cast my anchor to an outgoing tide.

Dragon's Breath

My life is structured.
Five o'clock, the whistle blows,
one hour later, I'm home.
One half hour of news and two beers,
then dinner, that's when we all pray for peace.
Hannah, two latently hostile teenagers,
and me is not so bad. After dinner,
kids' choice for two long hours.
They choose vampires, werewolves,
ghouls, children possessed, flying
and ground-bound dragons.
The pestilence is endless.
10 pm, they sleep. 11 pm, we sleep.
Now come night dreams of Ninja assassins,
tigers from the dark, coiled snakes with
flipping tongues, gaping lizards of every
description. I cannot diminish the night.

6:30 am, I am shaving and admiring
the green snake slithering up my arm,
and the flickering flames of hell on my chest.
After breakfast, I drop the kids off at
their bus stop and head for work.
How can I worry about Israeli peace,
African AIDS, malaria, and global warming,
when Armageddon is so close at hand.

An American Criminal (For Will C)

Born in a part-time craphouse
                where demons raped
his state of mind.

                He stepped with a street swagger
and hard-core mask that
                made his 'hood life hip.

As a popular pimp,
                he almost married his first girlfriend
but didn't have room in his stable
                so he turned her out.

Will C was schooled early to never
                trust politicians or preachers,
swore only on hard cash,
                thick ass and loaded pistols.

When hell came down on Will C,
                there were no deals to be made.

Police in the community were
                quick to claim victory over crime
one more time
                when they shot him down.

But there are no promises
                America can make
that will keep hustlers like Will C
                created by hungry streets
from going bump in the night.

An Offbeat Singer

Aretha Franklin and my
　　　　　mother sang in tandem from my

mother's bedroom on the weekends
　　　　　but the radio volume drowned

her out as she took
　　　　　care of her bruises.

My mother was always offbeat
　　　　　never had the soothing words for

five children's wounds after our father's
　　　　　rampaging visits petrified

our home on 1020 Vine Street.
　　　　　When she reached the crescendos of

her fallen notes of muted groans
　　　　　we could not hear her above our screams.

Last Night at The Blue Room

On that night, everyone
Calvin ever loved (or knew)
showed up at The Blue Room,
almost all of them
with someone else.

Pale Elizabeth E. came with a black flautist,
and she had an arm length cast
from her elbow to her left wrist.
A redhead, she wore pink. He sat in.

Hallie came with her camera and took shots
of the band, her hair dyed sharp and flat, piano key black.
She came with a group of young painters and sculptors,
men with black hair, dressed in all black.

And there were lots of girls he never knew
or thought he never knew. Memory slows.
Memory goes. Who knows? But women remember.

Z came, in honey-colored dreds again.
When she sat, it was like a light
came from her face. She was the sun,
a Sanskrit song; when lights dimmed,
a star. She sat alone. No one moved in.

Raylene came with her six kids, drove, in
from Manhattan, the Little Apple, and asked
to sit in on violin, "fiddle," and did.
She whispered, as she stepped from the stand,
her song done, "I'll always love you.
Now you go sit in," and Calvin did, for all
of those women, he did, and he didn't

do too bad; out of practice, but full of spirit,
like Z, for three songs he, too, lit up the room,
like a blue neon sign in a hot KC night
on the corner of 18th & Vine, he did.

In Her Parachute-Silk Wedding Gown

She stands at the top of the aisle
as on a wing. The white paper
carpet is cloud
spilled out. The pillbox hats

turned to her are the rows
of suburbs she falls into.
She is our mother,
or will be, and any of us

stumbling upon this scene
from the next generation, would fail
to notice what makes even her
tremble, with her silver

screen notions of marriage—
where all husbands scold
to hide their good natures, and wives
are passionately loyal.

Her groom, after all, is just a boy
home from the war,
his only trophy, the parachute
she's made into her dress. It's a world

of appetites, she knows
all too well, waiting there
watching the flowers
bob in her hands, dizzying.

Despite herself, she's not thinking:
Go slowly, pace it,
a queen attended to court,
Bette Davis. Nor of the $20 bill

her mother safety-
pinned to her underpants.
But: My God,
a room full of men, looking,

each will ask me to dance —
your hand tingles
when you touch their close-
clipped heads. And the men,

nudged to turn around
and watch the bride descend,
see a fellow parachutist
as they all drift

behind enemy lines,
stomachs turned over as they fall
into the horizon, into the ring
of small brilliant explosions.

Done

And then the white gloves fold the flag, falling
snow shut inside, and hand it to my mother-in-law,
good gray coat, fifty-two years married.
Too late now. Where silence ends, it stays.
He never told his children he loved them
or touched them with affection, except a scouring
of the head, or when grown, a handshake,
a tap on the arm. He never apologized.
He couldn't recite Shakespeare, wouldn't stretch out
with an espionage novel or sing in a piano bar
tunes from *Gigi*. He played the accordion
and with his wife at weddings led a polka
expertly among the quick couples, his face

nearly flickering with pleasure. When he read
it was the Stevens Point *Journal*, sales
and obituaries. He learned a trade.
He didn't go to college, or to high school.
Sent off as a farmhand at 12, he sent money home
that couldn't save the farm. And once in 1935
he watched all night from an open freight car
the billowing immaterial of the Northern Lights.
He didn't spend the war at a desk job,
perfecting pranks on the base's P.A. system.
He didn't break down, never lost a job.
He measured twice and cut once. He built
a house, he built a bigger house.
He was foreman, he was union.
He never took his children to the circus
and riled the lions with his echoing roar.
He didn't climb the trellis to the porch roof
and wail in the windows at his wife.
He never watched his sons pitch little league,
or appeared in the stands at wrestling matches,
or bragged about them at bus stops.
He was an officer in the St. Joseph Altar Society.
He paid cash for all the weddings
of his daughters he didn't encourage,
and he didn't stagger around the motel pool
in his socks. And in later years if he won
a few hands of pinochle against a visiting son
he might begin to talk, matter-of-factly,
about Omaha Beach, June 9, 1944,
his company of engineers landing
where the surf was still bobbing, the sand
still festering with burst cartons of bodies,
and over them he lugged his gear, fuel lines
for tanks, fresh grease for the machines.

Death Gets into the Suburbs

It sweats into the tongue and groove
of redwood decks with a Tahoe view.
It slides under the truck where some knuckles

are getting banged up on a stuck nut.
It whirls in the egg whites. Among blacks
and whites spread evenly. Inside the chicken

factory, the Falcon 7X, and under the bridge.

There's death by taxi, by blood clot, by slippery rug.
Death by oops and flood, by drone and gun.

Death with honor derides death without.
Realpolitik and off-shore accounts
are erased like a thumb drive lost in a fire.

And the friendly crow sets out walnuts to pop under tires.

So let's walk the ruins, let's walk along the ocean
and listen to death's undying devotion.

The Future Is Now

> *Under a new budget proposal from [Michigan] State Sen. Bruce Casswell, children in the state's foster care system would be allowed to purchase clothing only in used clothing stores.*
> -- Todd A. Heywood, *The Michigan Messenger*, 4/22/2011; http://tinyurl.com/3wkj7m3

Foster children deserve only
cast-off clothes: not a line from
Dickens, but from you, our leaders —
tailored suits and perfect teeth —

shoes to be polished soon by orphans,
chimneys swept by ragamuffins,
debtors sentenced to long drudgery in
sunless, airless rooms,

moldy cheese for the poor, their water
foul, lives cut short and yet too long,
while you sit down to roasted goose —
such is your dream.

But look, already the people press
their noses to your windows, they can't
afford a future, their bellies are empty,
their hands filled with stones.

Dust

In a tight house, a sealed room, it still gathers.
Some carried by winds from Stonehenge, the Vatican,
Marrakesh, atoms from graveyards and pyramids.
It falls into the stew, and we dine on pharaoh,
sphinx, the Pietà. Some arrives from space, two tons
every day, and perhaps brings alien bacteria to our guts.
The bulk is our own death; we shed tiny wafers of skin
into the common air and cannibalize one another,
every meal a communion. I sup tonight
on molecules once part of Poe's brain, Cleopatra's
fine breast. I detect hints of absinthe and venom.

1968

Each morning, punctual as a commuter, I left the hotel. I ate breakfast standing up at a counter inside a café and for the next three hours wandered the maze-like streets behind the Piazza San Marco. Hopelessly lost, in a pleasant daze, I followed one street after another, turning on impulse because the street looked inviting, because my feet propelled me that way, because my nostrils in the damp air detected a different smell. Sometimes I found myself at a dead end. Sometimes I came upon tiny squares with prinkling fountains, doorways arched with ornate designs, old women dressed in funereal black sweeping the entryways. Sometimes, by sheer chance, I came out on the piazza near the spot where I had entered.

After lunch I rested and read. Every afternoon at four I was back on the piazza. A dull February sun, glimmering between gloomy clouds, gilded the damp stones. The people sitting in the open-air cafés drank coffee and glasses of pink aperitif.

There was one event by which I regulated my internal clock every day. Precisely at four o'clock a little man in blue overalls emerged from a side entrance to the Doge's Palace, dragging two red canisters toward the shady end of the piazza. He stood stiffly at attention until all the bells in the churches and campanile tolled the four o'clock hour. Then he picked up one of the canisters and poured out a ribbon of tawny-colored seed, tracing a wide pattern as he walked.

Pigeons fluttered from the sky like ashy snowflakes. Tourists clutching cameras closed in on the whirling birds. Somewhere in the middle of this feathery riot, the red canisters bobbed up and down. Pigeons stacked three and four deep on the piazza crawled and shivered on each other's backs. Children frolicked about the fringes of this seething mass, kicking at the birds, sending them clucking into the air. The little man bearing the empty canisters strode out of the storm, pigeons clinging to his sleeves and shoulders like scraps of paper. Within a few minutes that corner of the square was picked clean. The pigeons melted back into the dreary sky, or settled along the eaves and balconies of the fancy buildings. A few remained, scouring the cracks between the flagstones.

That winter in London's Grosvenor Square, riot police standing shoulder to shoulder behind a phalanx of plastic shields hurled tear gas canisters to break up a protest in front of the ugly white monstrosity of the American Embassy. In Paris a few weeks later, demonstrators surged through the streets, tipping over automobiles and setting them ablaze. They tore up paving stones and chucked them through plate-glass windows. They clashed with right-wing groups shouting "Kill the Vietcong!" in violent battles that left scores of people stunned and bleeding. It was as if the world had taken its cue from those fervent monks who periodically torched themselves in the public squares of Saigon. Martin Luther King's assassination was more than a month away, but you could feel it in the air, the probability that anything could happen, countless deaths by senseless fire, the whole world convulsing before your eyes. How soothing it was to spend time in Venice, adrift in a floating gallery of finely wrought architecture, not seeing any cops, getting lost in the streets, listening to the melodious lilt of the language, taking the vaporetto out to Lida Beach, watching the oily water of the interior canals rise and fall to the tug of the moon.

After the little man in blue coveralls with the red canisters had departed from the piazza, I bought several packets of seed. In a corner of the damp square, away from the tables and chairs, I poured seed onto the brim of my Trilby hat and scattered it across my shoulders and sleeves. The pigeons settled in feathery clusters on every part of my body, pecking, snatching, gurgling with feverish rapture. I extended my overflowing palms and cackled giddily as they mewed and shivered the length of my arms. They settled on my shoulders, pecked my neck and fingers, clawed my wrists and elbows, tore at the loose threads curling off my tweed jacket. I was like a scarecrow, pocked with holes, sightless, tongueless, relishing every bold stab. The Venetians ignored me. People came to Venice from all over the world for every conceivable reason. What was this to them? For me, it was the best therapy I could think of. A kind of feathery immolation...scaly feet, thorny beaks...Osiris devoured by a rabble of tawdry birds.

I slept better than I had in months. Images of the Tet Offensive, stacks of American and Vietnamese corpses, which the BBC aired every night and which I watched on the scratchy black and white telly in my little flat in West Suffolk, faded from consciousness. The world was lit with fire, each fire igniting a fresh one, until, like a string of incendiary beads, they linked the hemispheres in a crackling necklace. Che Guevara was dead, so was a kid I'd gone to high school with, killed by a shellburst at Da Nang. Venice floated like a gaudy platter on the swell of a filthy tide. At night, half-drunk, prowling the clammy flagstones, I felt the city tugging at the ropes, as if trying to cut loose and sail out to sea. The dull roar of heavy bombers delivering their loads thundered in my ears. It was like being from no country at all, or a place you no longer belonged to, or wanted to have anything to do with. When people asked where I was from, I said, "Canada."

We Are All Immortal in August

The days are like geologic epochs,
the air like the weight of an inland sea.
Marsh hawks swoop over prairie dog towns.
Buffalo piss murky streams, roll in the muck
to rid themselves of flies. It's time to pierce,
to greet God at the point of a stick.
Libby Custer parades naked across
the quadrangle at Fort Wallace
to the cheers of her husband's subalterns.
Sentries in wool caps fire their rifles in salute.
Coyotes serenade her with melodious yips.

In the Tall Grass of a Landing Zone

The pup scents for the far
drop from the covey rise

so I fetch the last bird
down. Shot at close range

the little hen has come
apart. Her feathers,

wet with her blood,
cling to my fingers.

I probe for the femoral artery
where fragments

of his jungle fatigues
penetrate through the wound.

After it's over,
and for a long time,

I pick at my fingers —
threads in congealed blood.

On my knees, beside the creek
I wash the feathers away.

Counting Boys in a Truck

Phouc Vinh, 1965

The big deuce-&-a-half
skids to a stop
near a row of rubber
trees inside our Michelin
plantation camp.
In the cargo bed,
a tangle of arms & legs —
yellow roots torn
from their sandy,
red soil.
We unload 34 bodies
side by side,
display 14 AK47's,
8 bandoliers of 7.62
ammo & 2, 60mm mortars
in front of the dead.

The Captain invites
the press, inspects
his night's work:
Some in loin cloths —
Vietcong.
Some, black shirts — *Vietcong.*
Some naked & without
pubic hair — *Vietcong.*
I take shots with my 35mm.

The old slides are cached
inside my footlocker
in a corner of my basement
with 3 sets of jungle fatigues,
1 pair of boots, my dog tags,
5 punji stakes,

1 Montagnard's brass bracelet,
1 lock of raven-black hair
& 1 sculpted ivory Bengal tiger
I hustled from an old man on
Tu Do Street.

In Caravaggio's
St. John the Baptist in the Wilderness,

These were the lofty figures of his soul
— Anthony Hecht

the boy, pensive in his solitude, considers
his soiled foot and nails — the perilous paths
untraveled. Yet, it is the dance inside
his mother's womb and the prophesy
of redemption from Zacharias' astonished
tongue, that steady him. He carries the reed
like a quill, prepares to mark the straight
way through the desert with Jordan's ink.
Sunlit, in the tawny warmth of youth —
slant of light, fold of robe, long-shafted reed
and angle of repose — all this weight. Soon,
proclamations, baptisms, the choreographed beheading.

St. John the Baptist in the Wilderness *is in the permanent collection of*
the Nelson-Atkins Museum in Kansas City, Missouri.

Fifty Years After the Korean War

He sits before me like an ancient piece of glass,
swollen about his ankles,
shoulders thinned and brittle as piped cane.

We do not kill crickets
he croaks to no one in particular,
and the ensuing silence hangs
shroud-like between us.

You used to be a Marine
I want to tell his palsied fingers.
You sailed across oceans and wriggled
on your belly through brambled weeds
and spent shells.
Do you remember?

I am assured that you do not.

Once upon a time, before lameness
and milky-eyed stupor, in foreign fields and
post-adolescent terror you strained
to hear the silence of the crickets,
a hush that marked the unseen approach
of a faceless enemy.

We do not kill crickets, you say again,
the tenor of your voice no more
than a cracked plate.

Mind Trades Shadows with the Clouds

A neighbor's horses have been
moved to the field outside my study —
seven chestnuts, their shades of brown
blending, parting, forming new
densities of brown. They drift
across their acre like a slow-moving front.

At times I've had the unfamiliar
sense my life has walls I can
run my hands along in the dark,
a dwelling I seem to have to myself
at last, its astonishing silence,
my quarrels with former selves
having faded to an occasional
skirmish. I assume nothing.

Even through closed eyes I can see
the land filling with shadows,
and endlessly above it, light
older than anyone can imagine collides
without dissolving against
whatever appears in its path.
Some change is gathering beyond
where I can see, its shadow growing long,
unrecognizable, before a lowering sun.

To the human eye, the drifting horses
have nothing to do with the freewheeling light
above us. But if their legs allowed them
to lower themselves and doze
too long, whole worlds
would tip to destruction — the veins
and gut with their intricate barters

of gasses and proteins, the alto pipes
through which oxygen rearranges itself
into carbons, the tireless furnace of the heart.
Their brown backs soak up the November sun
which calms them—they have hardly moved
for the last hour, though if spooked they would
explode into their long history of flight.

Prayer

When I walk into this desert, a sea
of sand where mineral
waters gave up, the brown
swells don't fill me with praise
for the God I was raised on.
The sand presses into my palm
its story of breakage
and waiting. The slow work of
wind. Silences longer than lifetimes,
pauses. I turn to the sun
and away again, drinking
a little at a time. I trace
a lizard's tracks and think of
the people who first came here,
built fires at night, and drew the next
step of their journey in the sand.
I wash the dust from my mouth
but not the browns and tans
from my inner eye, not the braille
from my palm, not the heat from my skin,
not the dryness that peels off
and gathers again, bits of myself
adrift over the earth's face.

By Night, Penelope

unstitches the shoreline, the sea, the barely
visible mountain — all that binds her
to her halted story and to the suitors
who dwell below her chamber,
banging their goblets and cursing.
She unstitches the lambs being driven
single-file towards the banquet table.
She unstitches her flesh so that it rises, freed
from its single allegiance, the marriage bed
that would hand her like a birthright
to one of the next ones circling,
waiting to be chosen. She unstitches
their tunics while they sleep and piles them
like sand over the wine-drugged bodies.

She pulls jeweled threads from the sunrise
and later from amethyst twilight
and adds them to a garment all her own,
a cloak of breath, silk, all the hues
of weather, a cloak that bears her aloft
on what will later be understood as the beam
of meditation — each night she is swift
and ambrosial, her tears sweetening the torn
fields, the blood-dark seas, Cyclops' cratered eye.
Sometimes, from the depths of his own stupor
far away, Odysseus hears a curious singing or keening
that would press him towards a boundary
he cannot yet imagine, between his headlong quest
and the apparent stillness of the earth's flanks and inland waters.

1945

My parents were married the year
Europe cheered and returned
to the wreckage of her cities.
No hint of me beneath my mother's
flowered silk, the jaunty
shoulders—that dress lived
for tea dancing and long nights
on the town, officers on leave,
the muted brass of big bands
oozing caramel, as the sea
beyond Manhattan soaked up ash
and the rumbling of the last trains.

By the time I was born, Europe
was patched with old brick
and my father's Navy whites
hung in darkness, our nation quiet
at its borders. Every night at six
this family of four sat
down to dinner and smiled
through white teeth like TV people
while the dog who didn't know better
stalked other dogs in neighbors' yards.

By the time I was born
the schmaltzy music had faded away.
Everyone slept eight hours a night.
I came into the world
without a single memory.

Thirteen Pictures of a Sister

My sister feeling like the big china doll
from my mother

My sister in a red velvet dress
singing "Da—goo Da—goo" for home movies

My sister practicing a dance in black tights
boys watching through the porch window

My sister at the dinner table caught in a lie

My sister smug at the door with my boyfriend

My sister's face red and wet above the clothesline
I slapped her

My sister at my wedding thinking it was hers

My sister a beauty queen
a chiropractor's wife

My sister saying "I always thought if anything went wrong
with your marriage, it would be your fault"

My sister New Year's Eve: "We're having a party —
we didn't think you'd fit"

My sister at the Yoga camp talking to her latest
pretending not to see me sitting on their blanket

My sister giving me a painting saying "See
how lone, how sad? It reminds me of you"

My sister in her dome in the woods, her Taurus glass
bathroom, her kids, and a Taurus friend saying
"See how we live?"

Prufrock Was Wrong

Cecilia is resigned
that another man will leave her
to be "free to love all women."
I know she thinks if she's so beautiful
how come she's alone.
I have Greg who loves me
even though he knows me.
I take it in, feel very solid — very lucky.
And then fall in love with a Persian
whose dark eyes light up
when I enter a room.
And Cecilia leaves Carl for another potter
whose blue eyes light up
when she enters a room.
What we have here is a series of eyes
lighting up in a room.
Prufrock was wrong.
This is the way the women come and go.
They never mention Michelangelo.

Dear Mother, I Will Never Be Enough

I.

As an infant I will not know how to cry to tell you I am hungry.

When I am 3 I don't clean my room well enough to please you.

When I am 4 my sister looks like you and I look like my father.

When I am 5 bullies throw rocks and chase me home and you ask me
what I did.

When I am 7 I take money from your purse for the school charity
and a candy bar for me.

When I am 8 I know I am not you.

When I am 9 I know you are not me.

When I am 10 I try to tell you but it gets blurred and I forget.

II.

When I am 12 I sing in 4 church choirs and the Bay City Chorus
which you direct.

When I am 13 I am guilty of at least 3 days of the wrong attitude
though I make secret lists to avoid fights.

When I am 15 and leave instead of scream, you hiss my name to
come home and I obey.

When I am 16 I never tell enough of my sex life, though you ask
every afternoon.

I will never straddle a cello as well as I straddle a man.

I will never wear a dress that moves you to say how lovely I am.

At 19 my fiancé walks out and you scream that I forgot to take meat
pies from the oven.

The night before I marry you call me cruel and kick your feet and
pound your hands on the floor.

When my son is born you fly to my sister and leave spilled meat pie
in my oven.

When he is 7 I leave my son with his father.

Woman Found in an Art Gallery

I soothe myself on Kline's wide rocking chair brush strokes.
I learn to dance like Franz Marc's "Red Deer" arching their long
   necks.
I am as supple as the bronze woman "Ile de France."
I move like Jackson Pollock's swirls with liquid pauses.
I am as unselfconscious as Degas' "Woman Bathing,"
as unafraid of being plain as his ladies trying hats,
as casual as Cassatt's "Lydia Leaning on Her Arms."
I do not mind posing as Renoir's "Large Bather."
When I make love my bones go soft like Tanguy's "…Risk of the
   Sun."
In my person I see every angle of Charles Ross' "Prism."
I am "Infinity Light," "Hybrid Form No.1."
For each person I have loved Louise Nevelson makes a niche in
   wood.
I am one of Miro's "Women at Sunrise"
whose head tilts at a right angle
when I know what I mean.

Conquistadors

Six years have passed since she disappeared. Only legends keep her alive, tales from traveling Indians that speak of a fair-eyed child who dwells among a band of monkeys. When the General hears the stories, he summons the teller to his tent. If the story has a recognizable shape, he pulls out his parchment maps, which the Court Cartographer expands season by season, and fiercely examines his guest.

Here? No? Further west? A little north? Where exactly are you from, Grandfather?

The General burns with faith that the girl is alive, and his faith grows stronger with each passing year until we who remain are summoned. *Leave your weapons,* the general says. But only fools would enter the forest undefended.

How are we to make our way without them, I inquire?

She has lived in this forest for six years without benefit of a sword.

If she lives at all, I think but do not say. For I believe the child lives on only in the General's imagination....

All around us foliage drips and sighs. I pray that she will divine our presence and part the thick green curtain, rejoicing at our arrival. Ferns stand taller than the tallest man, vines rise up thick as thighs. I send my sword arms ahead to clear a passage. We stumble through this tunnel until we reach a strange, level space where the canopy has thinned to reveal the sun. For kilometers we've traveled without such light. Exhausted, my swordsmen sink to their knees, and I motion for the others to rest. A menacing choir of monkeys chatters overhead while I creep to the edge of our path. As suddenly as they started, the monkey voices stop. I strain to see through the leaf wall. The boy Pepé fidgets, and I put out my hand and catch his sleeve while the General's words ring threateningly in my ears: *Whatever you do, bring her back without a scratch.*

Something's there, Pepé whispers.

Do not move, I say. *And do not hope too much.*

An enormous fern sways. A small monkey sails upward into the trees as two drop down, swallowed by leaves. Suddenly, capuchins fly through the air, performing a dazzling acrobatic show, and we do not see her at first. She has stepped through the wall, shielded by a thin tissue of leaves. Monkeys hang off her like ornaments. A capuchin crouches on her head, another on her left shoulder, a third curled in her arms like a human infant, while others chatter from the *liana*.

I grip the boy's sleeve. Heat beats through our padded leather tunics, through air so thick with water we could drown. Fingers of light slant through the steamy air while rivers of sweat run down my head and into my eyes, distorting my vision. Beside me the boy Pepé grows agitated, his fingers diving at insects that creep under collars and cuffs.

The girl steps into the clearing and walks toward us. The child's face beneath the tangle of hair is still fair and more heart-shaped than I remember. She would be twelve now, not six. The eyes are so watchful her brows seem to form a cowl, like the tiny monkey in her arms. Her nut-brown hair flows over her back and arms, matted with twigs, flecks of moss, dried berries and a single blooming flower.

I finger the silk net we've carried so far—the General went to great lengths to have it spun. The world falls silent except for the pounding of my own frightened blood. The girl moves slowly but with purpose as if familiar with each frond and twisted trunk. Overhead, macaws blast their wild notes. Behind us, a jaguar screams, and Pepé falls to his knees. Birds of heaven, parakeets, toucans, and brilliant quetzals swoop through vines and down the thin columns of light. Mute and ragged, we crouch beneath these ruby-breasted, emerald-winged creatures.

The boy clutches one end of the net. His coarse breeches appear more patched than I remember, his white sleeves soiled to the color of skin. I dare not look down upon myself. I raise my hand: When it drops, the men will fling the net and encircle the girl. Like fishermen. Fishers of men, of lost children.

The men wait, disoriented by the forest's indifference. I fear their tension will speak directly to the forest while I ponder the distance between the girl and the net. Then a mosquito bites, an insignificant prick that feels like an affront. Foolishly, I let my hand fall, squandering the General's trust. Miserable with waiting, the men raise the net, form a hoop and throw it in one ineffectual toss. At this very instant she catches my eye.

We fall into noisy confusion. *Where?* Pepé leaps frantically into the air as the canopy fills with monkey shrieks. The capuchin troop swirls over us, turning the air muddy like carp stirring a pond. Pepé runs forward like a madman, leaps again and falls to the ground, his arms filled with a bouquet of leaves. When he finally lifts his hand from the foliage, we stare. He is holding a shred of linen that might once have been a hem.

Overhead the host of tiny monkeys raises the girl into the trees, higher and higher until she is gone. All that remains is the impenetrable green roof. Pepé clutches the remnant in both hands and weeps and looks in the direction she has disappeared.

We saw her, didn't we, Captain?

I put my hand on his shoulder. *You may tell the story if you like.*

I signal our retreat, and the monkeys' chattering stops. We hear instead a wood cricket's intermittent chirp as the forest encloses us in its breathing walls. I am suddenly afraid of the tall ferns that hide eyes, the liana hanging like staircases, the damp breath of this place that whispers, *Who are you...?*

Papa Cayo

Arriero from my village, north of here,
I come with my two good burros,
surefooted and gentle, descending
the volcano to the rocky plain below,
tin pans, ladles, cups, and hand mirrors,
all packed tightly in bundles that shake
like the humps of camels side to side.

In Tierra Caliente it is always summer
as I arrive among the Indians who take me in.
They remind me of my children at home, trusting,
but smarter than me, they speak like birds.
And me, beardless, slant eyes, speaking
coarse Spanish, I could be their cousin
or long-lost cousin come home.

We have a drink they make from some
local tree. It is sweet and cool
(after days through mountain passes
and scrub hills) like dark shining well water.
Perhaps it is their water
scooped from flowers flared like horns.
Perhaps that's why their voices sing.

I spend days at first listening to their elders
who talk of such things as the end of the world.
And when I see the stars at night
exploding into darkness, I believe.
The one called Josiah sits stoking the fire,
feeling his way to the end of his words,
the fire seeds he tosses searing the air.

Nights pass and what's here spreads patiently
each morning: forests mixed with fog,
dawnlight yawning over thatched roofs,
globes of ovens smoking with green wood.
My goods spread on the ground are poor handworks
beside the gifts they bring to me, among them
a white conch shell from the sea no one remembers.

Before the rains come I turn homeward.
Tall veering arcs of rain, they tell me,
rainbows of rain filling the sky,
pouring freely over the village,
over the village and then the world.
I have seen it only in dreams,
but it is the same, the same.

We say goodbye. Each time
I have to think not to hug these people
but stretch my hand and say *Luck* or *God bless.*
And each time they reach out,
and with one shy finger calmly touch
the palm of my open hand
as if the soul were nestled there.

Nacimiento

I was born late in the year,
at the hour when the stars
are bejeweled fish angling
across the sky. I was born
first son on a Saturday,
seventh day, Saturn's day,
day of faiths. Distant blue
orb ringed in crystals was
my origin. I arrived into
chilly life with clumps
of frost tangled in my hair.

Did my mother say my name
or simply cradle me against
her breasts — her radiance
a cloud of light hovering,
her breathing a kind of song?
Did my father grab a quick beer
on his way home from the hospital,
shaping words to fit the becalmed
bounty at year's end? Or dizzy
with lack of sleep and the newness
of being a father, did he slowly
drive across nighttime silence,
drinking in the lights and future?

I'd like to know, for through
such small things run meanings
that catch up to this me writing the page,
if only they can be imagined
more surely than the truth.

On Monitor Street
an apartment waited,
uncrowned heads

coming into focus,
rough hands
swaddling me in words
that rippled through
the calentón's
honeycomb flames.

Now my fall into life
opens and ends the night.
Like a voice it moves inside
this house, emanating from
candlelight and whiskey shot,
urging me out to the threshold
of my porch, the step off into
lustrous space, stars swelling
and falling near through clouds,
a net of trees, midnight bells.

Old Men Playing Basketball

The heavy bodies lunge, the broken language
of fake and drive, glamorous jump shot
slowed to a stutter. Their gestures, in love
again with the pure geometry of curves,

rise toward the ball, falter, and fall away.
On the boards their hands and fingertips
tremble in tense little prayers of reach
and balance. Then, the grind of bone

and socket, the caught breath, the sigh,
the grunt of the body laboring to give
birth to itself. In their toiling and grand
sweeps, I wonder, do they still make love

to their wives, kissing the undersides
of their wrists, dancing the old soft-shoe
of desire? And on the long walk home
from the VFW, do they still sing

to the drunken moon? Stands full, clock
moving, the one in army fatigues
and houseshoes says to himself, *pick and roll*,
and the phrase sounds musical as ever,

radio crooning songs of love after the game,
the girl leaning back in the Chevy's front seat
as her raven hair flames in the shuddering
light of the outdoor movie, and now he drives,

gliding toward the net. A glass wand
of autumn light breaks over the backboard.
Boys rise up in old men, wings begin to sprout
at their backs. The ball turns in the darkening air.

The Gray Man

We are cutting weeds and sunflowers on the shoulder,
the gray man and I, red dust coiling up around us,
muddying our sweat-smeared mugs, clogging our hair,
the iron heel of an August Kansas sun pushing down
on the scythes we raise against it and swing down
in an almost homicidal rage and drunken weariness.
And I keep my distance. He's a new hire just off
the highway, a hitchhiker sick to death of hunger,
the cruelties of the road, and our boss hates
poverty just enough to hire it, even this old man,
a dead, leaden pall upon his skin so vile it makes you
pull away, the gray trousers and state-issue black
prison boots, the bloodless, grim, unmoving lips,
and the eyes set in concrete, dark hallways that lead
to darker rooms down somewhere in the basement
of the soul's despair. Two weeks. He hasn't said
a word. *He's a goddamned ghost*, I tell my father.
Light flashes from his scythe as he decapitates
big clumps of yellow blooms, a flailing, brutal war
against the lords of labor, I suppose, against the state,
the world, himself, who knows. When we break,
I watch the canteen's water bleed from the corners
of his mouth, a spreading wound across his shirt,
the way he spits into the swollen pile of bluestem
and rank bindweed as if he hates it and everything
that grows, a hatred that has roots and thickens,
twisting, snarled around itself. A lizard wanders
into sunlight, and he hacks at it, chopping clods
until dust clouds rise like mist around him, and then
he speaks in a kind of shattering of glass cutting
through the hot wind's sigh, the fear: *Love thine enemy.*
He says it to the weeds or maybe what they stand for.
Then, knees buckling, with a rasping, gutted sob
as if drowning in that slough of dirty air, he begins,
trembling, to cry.

I was a boy. The plains' wind
leaned against the uncut weeds. High wires hummed
with human voices in their travail. And the highway
I had worked but never traveled lay across the fields
and vanished in that distant gray where day meets night.

Airlifting Horses

Boy soldiers gawk and babble, eyes rapt
in what seems like worship as the horses rise
in the bludgeoned air. A brush fire is swarming
roads and highways, and the last way out is up

or a flatboat in the lagoon. We used to drop
the reins and let them race there, hurdling
driftwood, heaps of kelp, waves lapping the sand
in a lace maker's weave of sea and foam.

Now they're startled into flight, and the air,
stunned and savaged by the propeller's flail,
beats us back. Its sudden thunder must be a storm
their skins have for the first time failed to sense.

Cowering beneath the blades, we have cradled them
like babies, strapped them in slings strong enough
to lug trucks, and their silence is the purest tone
of panic. Their great necks crane and arch,

the eyes flame, and their spidery shadows,
big-bellied and stiff-legged, swallow us,
then dwindle to blotches on the tarmac
as they lift. The cable that hauls them up

like some kind of spiritual harness vanishes
from sight. Their hooves pummel the heavy wind,

and the earth they rode a thousand days or more
falls away in hunks of brown and yellow.

Even the weight of their bodies has abandoned them,
but now they are the gods we always wanted:
winged as any myth, strange, distant, real,
and we will never be ourselves till they return.

Kansas

Leaning against my car after changing the oil,
I hold my black hands out and stare into them
as if they were the faces of my children looking
at the winter moon and thinking of the snow
that will erase everything before they wake.

In the garage, my wife comes behind me
and slides her hands beneath my soiled shirt.
Pressing her face between my shoulder blades,
she mumbles something, and soon we are laughing,
wrestling like children among piles of old rags,

towels that unravel endlessly, torn sheets,
work shirts from twenty years ago when I stood
in the door of a machine shop, grease-blackened,
and Kansas lay before me blazing with new snow,
a future of flat land, white skies, and sunlight.

After making love, we lie on the abandoned
mattress and stare at our pale winter bodies
sprawling in the half-light. She touches her belly,
the scar of our last child, and the black prints
of my hands along her hips and thighs.

The Himalayas

The stewardess' dream of the Himalayas
followed her everywhere: from Omaha
to Baltimore and back, and then to Seattle
and up and down the California coast until
she imagined herself strapped to the wing
just across from seat 7A muttering
little homemade mantras and shivering
in the cold, stiff wind of the inexpressible.
It could hardly go on like this, she thought,
the unending prayer to nothing in particular
whirling around in her head while she held
the yellow mask over her face and demonstrated
correct breathing techniques: the point was
to breathe calmly like angels observing
the final separation of light from a dead star,
or the monk described in the travel book
trying to untangle his legs and stand once more
at the mouth of his cave. The stewardess
delighted in her symmetrical gestures, the dance
of her hands describing the emergency exits
and the overhead lights that made exquisite
small cones in the night for readers and children
afraid of the dark. As the passengers fell asleep
around her, the stewardess reached up to adjust
the overhead whose cone of light rose over her
like some miniature white peak of the Himalayas
as if she were a cave in the Himalayas,
the cave of her own body, perhaps, in which
she sat patiently now, looking out, waiting.

CPR

Like striking a flint down into a basket of tinder —
a little damp, which spark will take?

— — —

And the live oaks arcing over the lot,
and the door that hasn't opened
                              for a while, now,

the bouncer there in the narrow hall, the bass
heaving its waves against the inside wall.

— — —

The slim rush of a car passes
beyond the privacy fence, then —

nothing else. The voicelessness of the work,
the ache in his back. And now

— — —

here's our fire: a man still breathing
his breath
            into a dead stranger's mouth.

[The child's cry is a light that comes on in the house]

The child's cry is a light that comes on in the house,
when the street is empty and the trees are still.
The light in the window gives voice to the cry,

so when the windows are closed, we still know
her voice is pushing against the walls of her room.
Her cry: a light that comes on in the house,

quivering the filaments in the bulbs, lifting
her parents out of their beds in the dark; at times
a neighbor's light will echo the cry. Her voice

arriving from what seems to be nowhere —
from inside such a tiny body, it comes on
and on, that cry somehow filling the whole house

when her parents are sleeping, when the world
is sleeping. Like a lighthouse beam it swings around
and out of her body, flooding the window, a cry

emerging from inside a dream, a need or fear
she can't yet utter; all there is is her breath
pushing the cry, the light coming on in the house —
and her voice: a light planted deep in the cry.

In the Barracks: A Found Poem

They had been in town only for a few days when the hills began pricking into the barracks (which once had been university classrooms) with sniper fire. That night, they crawled to their bedrolls in the corners, the cold spilling through the rooms like silt. There were no sandbags, and the bullets kept arriving,

solitary and oddly quiet — splintering the floorboards, cracking the lintel, the heavy door, tapping around in the billowing dark for just a second — to catch somewhere and the room went dull.

At dawn, four of the men crossed the courtyard to the library; when they returned they were pushing carts of books. In an act of uncertain desperation, they stacked them as high as they could in the windows, and that night the bullets came smacking into paper,

where they stuck. In the morning, Knox took down one heavy blue book and opened it: a bullet, surprisingly cold to the touch, had burrowed into the pages, which he lifted a few at a time from around the embedded snub — until it fell loose.

The shooter could not have intended to punch out the letters that were missing, Knox thought, yet they were gone. But the book could still more or less be read without them,

and he liked knowing that a bullet's approximate penetration through a treatise on the history of Western Europe was 350 pages.

Pioneers: Smoky Hill River, 1889

Here, she said,
here and no further.
I'm tired in my bones
and winter's coming on.

He looked across the river,
saw the great adventure
shimmer, flicker, fade.

The stone house held
through floods and storms.
Solid and solitary
it gazed across the fields.

Their children grew up
restless as rivers, listening
to invitations from the wind.

One by one they left,
headed west to the mountains,
dizzy with freedom
in the clear thin air.

Memory's wider spaces
spread across the plains,
called them home.

Chiaroscuro

To blessed innocence
we are born in a rush of light;
the world, heavy and dense,
makes us wary of flight.

We are born in a rush of light.
The gradual slipping to dark
makes us wary of flight,
of arrows that strike their mark.

The gradual slipping to dark
instills in us the fear
of arrows that strike their mark
and shadows that creep ever near —

instills in us the fear
of a world heavy and dense
and shadows that creep ever near
to blessed innocence.

The Country Doctor

It stands beside the same old apple tree.
"The Grindstone" — by Robert Frost

I was flying the small helicopter a few hundred feet above the ground. Its blades spun just above my head. After miles of clear air, cloud and fog were starting to form and push me towards the earth. With every mile the muscles in my throat tightened like a noose.

I flew to hold clinics in small towns in Kansas and Missouri. Partly. But mostly I flew because I loved to fly — to be suspended between heaven and earth. I was Charles Lindbergh and Albert Schweitzer, rolled into one.

And from the air I could see deer foraging in the fields. I could see the sun sparkle on waves of oceans of corn and wheat. At night I could see the jeweled lights of the city pass underneath my belly like phosphorescent plankton.

People in those small towns weren't like people in the city. They were more like the people I grew up with in the mountains of North Carolina. Some had family farms, working the fields day and night. Others worked in small factories processing pigs and chickens, or making moldings and batteries. Some were third generation welfare. A few, single mothers at fifteen, would never make it over the poverty line.

Carburetor heat with visible moisture and low manifold pressure. Check. A quick 180-degree turn...and I was safe for a moment.

I'd flown the route a hundred times. I thought I knew every inch by heart. A few miles to the west of me a highway snaked south. So I flew along a wall of fog, turned south, and began to inch along about fifty feet above the highway.

The sides of the road were too sloped to land. And I couldn't land in a field because of standing water. To land on the road was death by truck. So I crept above the highway.

Then poles began to appear ahead. Each was draped with wires that crossed the road — *wires. The biggest killer of helicopters.* You couldn't see them until they were caught in your rotors and you were headed for the ground and a grave. *How do I get out of this alive?*

Then suddenly a farmhouse appeared ahead and to the right. It seemed to materialize out of the mist. At first I thought it was an illusion and almost passed it by. Then I saw a calf in the yard. Beside an apple tree.

Ease over the power line. Keep away from the tree and the calf. Kiss the ground with the skids... and mixture, mags, master... off. The rotor blades slowed to a stop.

My hands were white and trembling. When I opened the door my legs didn't hold and I fell to the ground on my back.

The house and yard were silent as death. For a moment the only sound I could hear was my own breathing. Then I could feel and move my limbs and see the still blades above me.

I stumbled to the door of the farmhouse. Before I could knock, a woman in a flour-sack dress with grey-green eyes set in a wizened face opened it. She offered me coffee, bitter and hot.

I asked if I could use her phone. She pointed to a relic on the table. The voice of the nurse came over the line, and I told her about the farmhouse. She paused, then said she knew where it was, four miles north of town. She came and picked me up.

Patients in the clinic were waiting. I told them I had a problem with the weather. Helen was there with her husband. He took her for trips in his car to remind her of who she was. *For better or for worse.*

Jim was there with his wife and daughter. I gave them the news of his brain tumor with his little girl playing on the clinic floor. *In sickness and in health.*

Those clinics died long ago. But sometimes I close my eyes and see that apple tree, with the calf in the yard. And the faces of Jim and his wife and little girl, innocent to the world that awaited them.

The Horseman

You have to begin where the horse is at.
              – Tom Dorrance

The woman came off the 19 hands Belgian and flew like a rag doll toward the floor of the arena. She hit the dirt with a thump.

He was worried at first to see no movement. He always looked for movement after one of them came off. But then she laughed and he knew she was okay. They whinny like that when they're okay. She shook the dirt off and trotted over to the Belgian, who acted like nothing had happened.

When people brought horses to the clinics for him to fix, he knew he couldn't fix them and he told them that. All he could do was make the people a little more like the horse.

Now he was headed home, with the drone of the truck and the whine of the wheels the only voices he heard. It had been a pretty typical clinic, with the middle aged women and their Friesians, huge battle horses bred for war. These horses just wanted to be horses.

But the women wanted something else. They wanted to be something else. There were the usual thoroughbreds who the owners wanted to be cowponies. And cowponies who they wanted to be dressage horses. And the high-dollar warm bloods they treated like magazine centerfolds.

One woman, the one who came off, was trying to make a saddle horse out of a Belgian. Her legs could barely reach around him. He was built to be a draft horse, pulling a wagon. But he learned the fatal truth, that he was stronger than humans. Any human and most cars.

Treat a horse like a horse, not a pet. Let him think it's his idea, then go with it. A horse is a zero pressure animal. Get response with respect. That was another one. He tried to tell them but they just didn't get it.

He was glad to be headed back to the ranch. Back to his wife and his own horses. This year would be a good year. He'd started twenty-three colts. Weather was good.

The gravel popped under the big wheels of the rig. The motor and transmission whined as the rig climbed the hill, torqueing to the left like they were built to do.

He pulled through the gate, and unloaded his horses. He fed and watered them. Then he parked the rig and headed for his house.

He walked up to the door, his boots a familiar rhythm against the planks of the porch. The screen door squeaked as he opened it.

She was there, smiling, calm in her eye. She walked over to him, and nuzzled his left hand as, ever so gently, his right hand stroked her mane.

After Frost's Grindstone

Having two legs and a mind of my own
I waddled my way into this world
ridden by the monkey of art.

I have ground out tunes
with joints creaking and clock racing
trading poems for pieces of heart.

And for what? For the unmistakable mist
in the eye, the catch of a breath, a sigh,
a tremulous voice, the hint of a smile.

MRI of a Poet's Brain

In this image
of your brain
I see each curve
in the corpus callosum,
curlicues of gyri,
folding of fissures,
sinuous sulci,
mammillary bodies,
arcuate fasciculus,
angular gyrus,
tracts and nuclei,
eyes and ears,
tongue and pharynx,

but not a single
syllable
of one
tiny
poem.

Tattoo Man

Hit broadside, the van
flips in the middle of Highway 50
and lands on its side.
Wheels spin while my husband
climbs through the exposed window
and disappears.
Frantically, his head pops up
like a Jack-in-the-Box
as he struggles to free
a large, middle-aged woman.
Chunks of jelly-like tissue and blood
dot the ceiling and seats.
Gasoline runs the streets
and surrounds the shattered glass.

Suddenly,
the tattoo man appears —
thirties, skinny, and arms covered
with bluish pictures.
He tries desperately to free the woman,
encouraging her the whole time,
while the paramedics tie their sterile gowns,
one-by-one fasten the ties of the other,
stretch on their gloves,
and adjust their goggles.

What We Need

It is just as well we do not see,
in the shadows behind the hasty tent
of the Allen Brothers Greatest Show,
Lola the Lion Tamer and the Great Valdini
in Nikes and jeans
sharing a tired cigarette
before she girds her wrists with glistening amulets
and snaps the tigers into rage,
before he adjusts the glimmering cummerbund
and makes from air
the white and trembling doves, the pair.

Taxidermy

Let us mourn the giraffe and zebra,
dead during heavy bombardment
in a Gaza Strip zoo —
one of terror,
one of tear gas.
There is no money to replace them,
so they will be stuffed
and put back in their cages
for children to see
how it was when these were animals —
although someone who can remember
will have to explain
how the brusque tails sent flies reeling;
how, like barley in an evening wind,
they bent their necks to water;
how the eyes were not glass then,
and darker.

Threads

She had lost her memory at 35.
"So what?" her husband always says, and smiles
when someone remarks. Tonight they've come
to hear B.B. King in concert, live, in Memphis.
They saw B.B. last year, but she can't recall.
Her husband reminds her of that evening now,
quickly moving them through the smoky crowd
so she can get a closer look. In perfect
patience and love, he seats her where she commands
a clear view of the stage, closing his hand
and opening it on the smooth back of her chair.
At the small table, their elbows touch.
On the stage, B.B. is resplendent in black
and baby blue. The husband asks his wife
if she remembers the color of the jacket
when they saw B.B. last. "Pink," she says.
It was orange. But he likes the way she touches his arm
when memory skims the surface of her mind
like, he imagines, the shadow of a gull
over sleeping water. His face burns
with the thought, the hope, that tonight in bed —
perhaps early, perhaps late — she will turn
to him and speak against his back, recalling
the jacket perfectly.

Telling Time

My son and I walk away
from his sister's day-old grave.
Our backs to the sun,
the forward pitch of our shadows
tells us the time.
By sweetest accident
he inclines
his shadow, touching mine.

from The Rufus Chronicle

> *You walk along the forest edge, you watch your dog, but all the time images and faces of the beloved, dead or alive, keep coming to mind... All your life unwinds as smoothly and swiftly as a scroll.*
> —Ivan Turgenev, *A Sportsman's Notebook*

JANUARY

Twelve autumns we traveled the fields together, and were prodigal with our time. Almost to the last we did not consider endings.

He flew the fences. I clambered ungainly over. He plunged boldly into the thickest, prickliest cover, while I took the easy way around the edges.

"The pup has *style*," a man once said, and I thought I'd won the lottery. He also had much courage, and a ruling passion. If I'd ever gone at writing with a dedication like that, there's no knowing what work I might have done.

"He'll live in his house outside," I told my wife when we brought him home. "He'll be a hunting machine." That lasted until the weather cooled. Then of course he joined us and the old dog and the cats indoors. He slept in a chair or beside the bed. But when we returned from an evening out and he met us at the door with that look of innocence, we knew there'd be a warm place on the covers where he'd trespassed. He could be devious. A sandwich unattended for a moment would vanish in a gulp. His lust for bagels was indecent.

But those were merely vices.

His abiding devotion was to the hunt. He marked the season's turning, and when the alarm sounded in the dark of a November morning, he always *knew*, and was waiting already beside the downstairs door.

His eyes, gold when he was young, deepened to chestnut brown. A knee failed and had to be repaired. He hunted on it eagerly as

120

ever, not seeming to mind the price of soreness afterward. Then the cataracts began to come, but it was his nose that brought the important messages, and the nose was still keen.

Nearly every man who ever walked behind him spoke of someday wanting a Rufus pup, and several had them or have them now. One of those was Fred Kiewit, who, in the year when we were in Paris saw to it that the autumn was not wasted. Fred is gone, too, now. As is that other fine man, Stuart Michelson, for whom Rufus pointed and brought to hand the last bird just at the mellow sundown hour of the last day Mitch and I had together. All of them — those men and Rufus — had full lives, good lives. And good lives never are long enough. But in the end there are some things that medicine cannot fix.

He passed his last night at home, on a pallet in the kitchen, with me beside him. He was tired, and had borne enough, and had been too good a friend to hurt any longer.

In the morning, then, I dressed for the hunt — put on my boots, and folded my canvas coat beside him, with the bird smell still on it. Also his leash. His head came up from the blanket. He'd have stood if he could. All the old excitement was in his eyes.

Dan, who'd cared for him so well from earliest puppy days, made the sad house call. Came to kneel with me beside him. And just as I let Rufus take the quail wing from my hand, released him to wherever it is that old gun dogs and those who've followed them finally go.

With my wife and daughter I drove to the farm, and on a day of false spring, working together under a warm sun out of season, we buried him, wrapped in the coat, facing a thicket in which he almost always found a covey.

My theology is a bit shaky, and I don't profess to know what, if anything, lies beyond the darkness. But I believe in covering all the possibilities.

So before we walked away, I looked a long minute straight up into the cloudless deeps of that sweet springtime sky and said, in my heart if not actually aloud, *Freddy, Mitch, I'm sending you a pretty good dog. But he isn't given, only loaned.*

ARCHAEOLOGY

In some future year, a different proprietor of the land, out walking on a fine spring day, may pass that way—along the abandoned fence row where the blackberry canes are white with bloom and the wild rose makes mounds of pink at the field's edge. That brushy line, in which no posts or wire remain, divides two meadows of native grass that fall away toward the dark of woods on either side.

The walker will discover, tucked in close against a thicket, a curious mound of flat fieldstones, too neatly placed and fitted to be accidental. Curiosity will bring him back there another day, carrying a shovel.

He will lift the stones aside and excavate beneath them, possibly imagining a treasure. But what he will unearth will be only the folded skeleton of a dog, and four large plastic buttons of the kind found on a canvas hunting coat. Also, if he looks carefully, the wing bones—finer than matchsticks—of a small bird.

If that man is a hunter, he will understand immediately what he's found. He will know that the creatures those artifacts represent are gone from there, away to some field of always autumn. I like to think he will replace the earth and stones, and leave the place as it was—a little cache of things that tell no story except when all together—safe again from rushing time.

Thanks, Robert Frost

Do you have hope for the future?
someone asked Robert Frost, toward the end.
Yes, and even for the past, he replied,
that it will turn out to have been all right
for what it was, something we can accept,
mistakes made by the selves we had to be,
not able to be, perhaps, what we wished,
or what looking back half the time it seems
we could so easily have been or ought ...
The future, yes, and even for the past,
that it will become something we can bear.
And I too, and my children, so I hope,
will recall as not too heavy the tug
of those albatrosses I sadly placed
upon their tender necks. Hope for the past,
yes, old Frost, your words provide that courage,
and it brings strange peace that itself passes
into past, easier to bear because
you said it, rather casually, as snow
went on falling in Vermont years ago.

Return to the Desert

The desert said nothing
when I left it long ago.
The great masters are still
the great masters and the giant
saguaros still guard their mountains.
The Gila monster lies so flat
against granite that he has become
a part of it, but his secret eye

watches me. No bird could spot him
and there's no need to fear a shadow —
it's just me, back again, standing
on the same sand, and pebbles
that were under my feet years ago
are still looked upon by those same
saguaros and rattling ocotillos.

I recall their long shadows
giving way to the alpenglow.
On cue the overture chirrs and howls
as the canopy of stars lifts into place.
The night chill speaks to our bones,
reminds us we must return to our burrows.
But I hope to keep faith with these creatures,
leave them in good hands, take not one stone
of their mountains, nor invite them to join
                    the madness of man.

To a Child of Baghdad

Our bombs may blast you
to a better life. You and your vivid parrot
may even change places. We give you
a chance, at least, to better yourself.

Who knows, you may be born beneath
a lucky star next time, maybe live
in our land of milk and honey,
and do some bombing yourself.

They say you'll die this year,
that our bombs did it — the power outage,
polluted water, that sort of thing —
but they're stretching a point.

If you knew these bombs you would love them.
We draw faces on them. We keep them spit-
shined and give them pet names.
And they are smart—that's how they found you.

Legacy

I did not inherit
a ship in a whiskey bottle
or even a square foot
of scorched earth
or one purple fuchsia
aspiring still by a stone.
And hence my passion has been
to leave at least something—
a coin from a distant land,
a hat that could fit
another head or a ring
worn on my hand.

And no doubt a portrait
would do, one where I wear
my foolish grimace—
half smile
and half bitter wince
of woe. I want some one
of you to know
it was hard, holding on,
that I did so—
though some days it was noon
before I could crawl out
to the light,
that I kept intact
my fool faith of a child.

Now I stand by the sea,
once small as a tub
facing the sky. And I know
that if I returned
to Grandfather's yard,
his round tin tub would still
be standing, its waters
trembling, going nowhere —
like the foreign sea, year
after year
with its ancient shores rusting.

After Tagore

Strange to think how we once had wings —
these very cells that make up our flesh,

so earthbound and heavy. And strange
to think we were dinosaurs and that

the water flowing through us back to earth
once flowed through them, and odd to think

that we were once tiny horses, great whales,
little bugs that scurry around on the ground

and have done so for millions of years. Strange
to think we were again and again newborn

babes just learning to smile. And the scales:
you once had scales, my love, and often

        delighted another snake.

_____**DEBORAH LINTON**

"Mannington, West Virginia, November 23, 1968 – (AP)"

It was like my grandfather's
Retelling his near disasters,
This headline. He survived three.
Each the more miraculously:
Once, he was in a lucky vein;
Another time, hayfever kept him home;
Another, like the good Chinese in myth
Who are yanked by their braids
From destruction, my long-legged Slovak grandpa
Was dragged by his shoes from a burial of rock.
We looked at the coal
Imbedded in his nails and studied
His hands' geography.
Each chip—visible as a scar,
Truthful as a callous—
Was romantic as a streetmap of Prague.

Train from the South

Another half-finished tale, another dream
my father calls with no beginning, no end.

He wants to tell me when he first heard
the words *Jim Crow*, a phrase rarely spoken

anymore, yet all that comes before or after
defined by it. He guesses 1937, a heat wave

in the north, the station's gravel-dusted windows
open to the oiled sky. The train late, his mother

impatient, reaching for a handkerchief.
Come here, sit down, she told him, but he pushed

past the standing lines and roped cases.
The train came in, at first a boy's dream

of metal and clouds, then as the last car approached,
something appeared he had never seen before — faces

from the fields of Mississippi, Alabama —
hot, parched faces of men crushed for air.

Why can't they breathe? my father, the boy,
asked his mother. The still heat, his mother patting

her face and hairline. The two words she spoke
in the train's slow halt. My father stops there,

hearing his mother's voice, hearing the phrase repeat.
How twinned they are, the dreamer and the voice.

Womanhood

She slides over
the hot upholstery
of her mother's car,
this schoolgirl of fifteen
who loves humming & swaying
with the radio.
Her entry into womanhood
will be like all the other girls' —
a cigarette and a joke
as she strides up with the rest
to the brick factory
where she'll sew rag rugs
from textile strips of Kelly green,
bright red, aqua.

When she enters,
and the millgate closes
final as a slap,
there'll be silence.
She'll see fifteen high windows
cemented over to cut out light.
Inside, a constant, deafening noise
and warm air smelling of oil,
the shifts continuing on...
All day she'll guide cloth along a line
of whirring needles, her arms & shoulders
rocking back & forth
with the machines —
200 porch-size rugs behind her
before she can stop
to reach up, like her mother,
and pick the lint
out of her hair.

Midwifery

Story is she had black eyes & crackling hair.
Once drove a fat pickup through national woods
and got jailed.
But smart, that one.
Did her midwifery off country roads,
far from the law.
Times she'd be on the road for weeks,
up at dawn, windshield lit pink,
tarmac pulsing like a brainwave.
Kept all the due dates in her head,
her jeans and underpants rolled in a bag,
a birthing apron looped on a hook in the cab.
They say school kids used to watch her work,
3 or 4 creeping in,
while someone's mother lay churning,
legs up to her chin,
and she rowing her, each stroke a heartbeat,
that midwife's arm,
a fast, quick oar pulling them both,
mother and child,
to wide soft sheets, the shore.
"Out!" she'd holler later
to the O-mouthed kids,
arm snapping as each face vanished,
and she paused,
apron washed & whipping on a line,
a white flag crossing & recrossing the horizon.

Faith

As my daughter
suckles, fleshy
fingers knead
and pull at the
white moon
of my breast.
She carries
instinct within
her. Stroking brings
a slow ache
in my chest,
a rush of milk.
But I believe
these caresses
are small affections.
Because what is love
if not hunger,
if not supplication?
And what is
love returned
if not provision?

The Fountain

– for RT

The fountain rises from a deeper place
and thrusts its liquid spear into the air
then turns to fall with death-defying grace.

But when we fall, we struggle to save face
and make our way with ever greater care.
The fountain rises from a deeper place.

Like the gymnast hurtling into space
who wraps around the trapeze in mid-air
then turns to fall with death-defying grace,

the falling and the rising interlace.
It's fear that holds us back from going there.
The fountain rises from a deeper place.

It's only life. Summer will replace
what Spring has cost. The tree will drop its pear
then turn in Fall with death-defying grace.

And so we fall into a hard embrace
and push our hips together in a prayer.
The fountain rises from a deeper place
then turns to fall with death-defying grace.

Reversing a Decision

So loud the wail of cicadas
you cannot hear

the dog barking or the cries
of boys in a sprinkler.

You cannot hear
your heels scuff the pavement

or the story being read
to a girl in a nightgown,

her head on the shoulder
of a father yawning

in the last house.
The sidewalk slides

into black. The moon
hangs, huge

in its noose of stars.
Branches brush

your throat. You cut
backward through the night,

returning to the insult
of a porch light, the husband

who knew before you did
that you would return.

Keeping Your Place

I am your bookmark
holding your place between sheets
while you arrange the forest
from your chair, your fingers falling
again and again onto the clacking
keyboard like rain on banyan leaves
until you double back to bed
in the late morning, encircling
my spine, slipping in where you left
off, finding your place to get lost in
the book so hard
to put down once opened

Wood Carver

You look for grain and texture —
like walnut,
or this piece of quartered oak.
Not sapwood, mind you.
Heartwood is what you want.
You can tell by the darker color.

And it needs to season.
Soaking in running water's best —
right after it's been cut.
Then you dry it out with wood smoke,
like the old carvers did.
There's pieces in English churches,
must be five hundred years old,
still sweet and solid.
Took time.

Still takes time —
if you want to do it right.

Encantation

Today is Wednesday —
the proper day to gather
periwinkles.
The grass is sweet in the morning air,
the sky is big
with thunderheads and interlaced
with golden threads of sun.
Yesterday was rain —
time to pick vervain.
The day before was blue —
day for bittersweet,
a day for rue.
But today is Wednesday.
Come.
Let's gather
periwinkles
today.

Fourteen-Word Sonnet

Star,
who
are
you?
Light
we
might
be?
One
more
sun. . .
or,
just
dust?

The Last Shot

Colt 45. M-16. Glock 19.
My brother and I watch *The History of Guns*.
Diagrams and battle scenes
explain the ways of war. I learn
the dominance of an Uzi, the clout of a Luger.
My brother points at guns he's owned,
before he oiled and wrapped each one
to send home with his sons, before
his doctors started another treatment.

Last summer I lined up with his children
to shoot a Coke can with his AK-47.
He insisted on where we pointed our toes,
pulled back our shoulders, slumping
under the rifle's heft. Whether we hit
dirt or can, we handed off the gun,
changed by the force of that bullet,
eager to see my brother shift and nod approval.

He wishes he'd taught me a better feel
for a trigger, the upper hand in the sight.
He thinks I should own
at least one gun. Snub nose. P-32.
The borrowed BB gun doesn't count.

On that summer day, he stood so small,
his head hairless, the perfect marksman
now a shadow leaning. With a patch
over one eye, he shot his last time,
the kick knocking him off his feet.
The war inside him using up his arsenal,
his t-shirt a white flag billowing,
he grabbed the side of the shed and hung on.

Ragazza

A good Italian woman
will cover her dust-free house
with crocheted doilies,
bear dark-eyed sons,
know what to do
with artichokes and chick peas.
Her floors will shine.
She will serve tender brucaluni
in her perfect sauce,
make her own cannoli shells,
make biscotti for every wedding.
Supper will be hot at six o'clock.
She will always wear dresses.
She will not balance the checkbook.
He can doze behind the paper
when she washes dishes.
Because she will never leave him,
he will forgive her bulging thighs.
Because he will never leave her,
she won't notice unfamiliar stains.

Italian men always know ragazzi
who work the fields of Bivona.
For airfare one will come.
In time she will learn English.
In time they may learn to love.

In the Same Place

I miss the man four tables over,
sitting alone, tapping his glass.
I miss the man waiting with notebook
in the class I never took.
I turn too late to the man in the gallery
admiring the same painting,
the man leaving the filling station,
his suit coat over his empty seat.
I miss the man jogging the footpath
an hour before I arrive,
the man four up in the theatre,
three aisles over in the grocery.
I miss the man standing
in his own backyard,
looking at the same April stars,
thinking about the woman
who took the other elevator.
Tonight when we turn alone in our beds,
the invisible one is half asleep on our pillows.
We feel the breath of the other.
For a moment our fingertips touch.

Wounded in Chu Lai

Under fragrant bait there is certain
to be a hooked fish   —Sun Tzu

Pieced together in a wobbly scrawl,
letters fragmented like an engine's
stuttering start. They describe
the Quonset Hut lined with faces
like choir boys, holding the open vowel.
You shiver under a sheet,
thinking of your men on the hill,
until the needle finds a vein.
Tubes drip blood and fluids.
The nurse debrides your open wounds,
plucking scabs, dead tissue,
shrapnel from the mine.
Morphined, you rocket
out of yourself, a ribboned pole
topped with a machine-gun nest,
spiraling up into stars. When orderlies
lift you to clean white sheets, a latexed
arm reaches down your throat, peeling you
inside out. At night, the ward
is a litany of moans, the drugged garble
of men sloshing through mud.
The bandaged soldier beside you
collapses into himself; Death
wrestles out the last glow.
On the ceiling, a platoon of helmeted
shadows march forward, jabbing air
with bayonets, grenade pins locked
between their teeth. The point man,
in crossed bandoleers, whacks
with a machete at your bandaged head,
a piñata filled with jungle dreams. Morning,
doctors check nerve damage. Their faces

melt into your platoon, caught in ambush,
calling your name for orders. "Fire,"
shouting, "Fire!" you rise through the brain's
short circuits, ricochet off walls
where spiders feed on each other,
tapping messages on a master web
that traps every wounded soldier,
hooked on the same line.

All the Time Running

Even when you see it coming,
leave tread prints behind,
you'll wonder about this moment,
this curve at dusk, the dog chasing
a coyote across a field, the coyote
losing ground each time he checks
his pursuer, all the time running
toward the road, toward the woods
on the other side, all of us thinking
we have enough time. Then brakes
yield that rubbery smell of trying.
In that instant the coyote sees you,
his eyes hold all he knows.
When you stand on the shoulder,
you'll see the pool form, the eyes
glaze over, the body heat
shimmer into air; how fast
light subtracts itself.

How It All Begins

How slowly the notion comes to you
working a little later every night,
how it might be to linger
and maybe find some noisy place
to let the evening settle down.
On a busy corner
you realize you're in the middle of a plan
you hatched without thinking.
You turn down a little side street
you've imagined taking
many times before,
head for a window blinking neon
where you can watch the evening fall,
where you won't be by yourself
with all those strangers streaming by:
where you can order up a drink
and feel the liquor work
and tip your glass
to every passer-by
and whisper to yourself
that the night has just begun.

Missing

What I miss now is what we both kissed off
so quickly once: my mother's decorator vase,
Grandpa's top hat, your scratchy 78s,
the framed photo of Aunt Kate
(now I wonder what she looked like)
that turquoise table lamp,
your father's only gift.
What we so easily dismissed
comes back: those long afternoons
when we kept company with the old bunch
under the ordinary elms
beside the peonies and mock orange,
watching the shadows grow enormous
with a drink or two, with cigarettes:
one almost forgets,
then recollects.
The green lawn chair
somebody (was it Ted or Wally?)
sat in and made wisecracks.
And the squeaky glider where Martha
(was that her name?) held court.
Missing, these old chums:
did they move away or were we remiss,
misplacing their whereabouts?
Why the whole damned parlor's gone
where your chair sat: remember the rings
beside it on the end table
from your cold Schlitz?
And my rocker that wore grooves
in the purple carpet,
that's missing, too,
and so am I
and so are you.

The Other

It was another
surprise: to have found you
speaking the same language
I speak, and for an hour or two
we saw things the same way
or seemed to.

You went to sleep first:
I watched you,
your breathing interrupted
by little fits
of dreaming
in that other country

I fell into soon
after, and if we dreamed
each other, each of us
was another — two others
having a few hours together
before falling

apart, into other landscapes.
Look, there you are across the park
beside the big elms, waving
and waving to someone and saying
what might be hello
or ta ta.

Like a Tree

The body owns us, lets us, inside it, live
and breathe through branchy sponges it provides:
the head covered with hairs like leaves,
the trunk's limbs sprouted
with fingers and toes like twigs,
and within, the heartwood's dark thuds
are the ax man's steps, which will bring it down,
this body with a head like a bloom,
and with inner petals, too, delicately tissued
purses and pods of sap and seed,
and the Adam's apple, the vocal chords and tongue
give us a voice which is the body's voice,
full-throated, words of the flesh,
unwrapped and uttered by way of bone and blood.
Only by the always-bodily thing are we
brought to what our brains conceive
before the body falls like a tree.

Other People's Fathers

My old man slept on the front porch
on summer afternoons in his plaid boxer shorts,
a beer warming by his side, arms dangling,
flailing in bad dreams:
I hung around the block, and never knew
I was hunting for another,
among other people's fathers,
but in every backyard or old garage
sober, puttering stand-ins
were willing and able, saw the kid
with unwashed face and a permanent whine
in sore need of some strong-armed

paternity: I would wander up to one
clipping hedges or staking his tomatoes,
and loll around, asking too many questions,
a sure sign I needed something,
and soon he'd turn to me, offering a grin
and winking to himself he'd suggest
a game of catch, a fishing trip, let me
go through the lures in his tackle box,
watching from the corner of his eye
for me to straighten up, for my questions
to cease, for my eyes to stop shifting
back and forth, but I couldn't stop my
wriggling curiosity, and I couldn't catch,
got his fishing lines all tangled until this
borrowed father began to wrinkle up his
eyebrows with a look that said I was beyond
rescue and turned back to his work, let me
float back home to my snoring father
who might wake up half-sober, smiling
weakly from his beery dreams, filled
with a wan, kid's eagerness,
his puzzled eyes, like mine, brimming over
with a million crazy questions
the calm, sober world could never answer.

from *Trinity*

He saw the sign for Ovid, Colorado, out of the corner of his eye as it swung past. His hands tingled with sleep. The overpass, he had been told, was about two miles north of the eye-blink town. He thought he would know the spot but didn't and went past the underpass almost to the edge of Ovid before turning around and coming back. He stopped the truck on the north side of the overpass and got out onto the shoulder. Wind moved the tough dead grass. He waited, leaning back on the cold metal of the truck, looking up at the white sky.

Before, in planning the trip, he had seen himself walking the shoulder of the road and coming up to the exact point of impact, finding glass and tire burns and ruts in the dirt. Why these things would be preserved for him after almost a year he didn't know. Anyway, the truth was he had no idea where the place was within the mile stretch of interstate.

He did not feel her near him until she stood up in the tall grass. Her hair was filled with the grainy heads of wild cane. She was dusty from sleep and crumbs of dirt sifted down the front of her shirt. Her eyes were wry, a normal expression. When she opened her mouth to speak, Milse found himself looking at the edge of a fence that had posts made of cut sandstone. These posts were shaped by the strong wind and some of the shapes were quite womanly. The one he looked at was not Emma. Emma believed in the trinity of the holy spirit and would never have left her soul to occupy a column of rock.

She had told him once before, in fact, that the trinity was their only real problem. "You don't believe in God," she said.

"I believe there's a God."

"But not a father, son, and holy ghost."

"No," Milse said. "None of that stuff."

"I see your trinity," she told him. She pointed to a stack of *Playboys* under his coffee table. "Your worship. A trinity of behinds and big boobs."

"It's the only thing I collect," he explained.

Emma never had understood his beliefs. Milse had proof of this within their first week of marriage. Right after their honeymoon, he had accidentally maimed a barn cat. It was asleep on the corn conveyor that carried the newly shucked ears up to the bin — a big, heavy calico with white feet. The conveyor was only on for a moment, but that was just long enough to pull its hindquarters in between the rollers. Milse had not named the cat. At the animal clinic, it seemed wrong that there was no name to put on the form he filled out. He tried to make one up while the vet's assistant hovered over him, but couldn't.

The vet — a young man about Milse's age — was surprised at Milse's expression when he placed the cat on the metal exam table and it moaned from the pain.

"It's a stray, didn't you say?"

"Yes. A stray."

But the cat had been there in the corncrib the day the realtor showed them around. When Milse had seen it, he had hoped someday to belong that much to the place. He had hoped the same for Emma. But Emma hadn't been calmed by the scene — the lazy-eyed stare of the cat, the salty smell of corncobs in the wood, the light in the cracks of the timber. He could never get over the feeling that she was there on a dare.

The vet put the cat down with an injection. Milse wasn't thinking clearly at the time and thought that the shot was an anesthetic. It didn't really come clear to him until the vet took off his glasses, pinched the red marks on his nose, and asked him if cremation would be alright. Milse nodded and walked out. He felt lightheaded. On the drive home, the road seemed to shimmer under the truck.

"I wish he had told me beforehand," he told Emma later. "I could have put it down myself."

"It only suffered a little longer," she said.

"I mean I could have put it down *here*."

Emma gave him an impatient look. She knew that he had his own beliefs in the aspects of the spirit. And just like hers, his beliefs made up the three sides of a trinity. He had not realized this until the death of the cat. And then Emma's. There was the first aspect, which departed into a dark beyond. The second stayed behind, tied to the nearest living spirit. The third occupied the place of death.

It was this third aspect that Milse could not really talk to Emma about. He could not tell her the reason for the sudden weight in his groin in the clinic or name the disappointment he felt at knowing that the spirit of a barn cat would not be occupying a barn....

Cameo

It's nearly impossible now for me to believe
you were my wife for awhile. You were fine
but not delicate, smallish but not fragile.
On the worst nights, I walk sleepless
through our house and look at objects.
There are many of these. I will reveal
only one: A cameo locket. I am compelled
to compare you with this thing, for it was
your silhouette I loved the most — that
sharp chin, pert nose, and if the curve
of a human skull can be called elegant,
yours was. The cameo does not stare
back at me; silhouettes do not do so,
nor do the dead. Near this object lies

a collection of Beckett's works (I keep
them both where you left them). When
you died, you were studying lines for
a part. It was that absurd play (but
aren't they all) where two characters
live in trash cans, and some nights
I would watch you as you read the thing,
clearly delighted. "Endgame," it was called —
and then yours came. Foolishly, I keep
looking for you, as if you were a lost charm
one might turn up in an odd place ...
but you are gone. You were my cameo,
my bas relief, my comic relief. You had
a brief part in my play. Didn't you?

The Knob

— for Michael

On left over days
I go to your room,
grasp the knob
on your door,
feel something of you
cupped in my hand,
left molded in metal,
chilled by the still,
resigned in the silence
held in this knob
the touch of your hand.

An Empty Barn

stands in Missouri,
a stone's throw
from a river. Vines climb
rafters where we cried
when Daddy cast
hurtful words with
the same ease he used
with his fishing line,
hooked the blush
of womanhood.
Wild flowers
bloomed at night,
moon flowers twisted
on a bob-wire fence.

Gestation

—for Sherry Lehn Curtis, 1977-1999, US Navy

In my life, I am midwife to horses
and I have blood to wipe from this dam's legs.
She gave birth last night.
I run hot water over towels.
I place them in a sterile ice chest
to hold in the warmth on this cold day.

It took a day just to figure out how
to clean her legs in this frozen time of loss.
I am sluggish of mind and limb
in this season without my daughter.

The new dam birthed a colt,
all red and white.
I want to clean my mare's legs,
I would that I could wash my spirit.

She gave birth,
as did I twenty-two years ago.
This white mare with few spots
comforts me, as I am spotted with pain.
What was I doing? Once again?
...to do this, for my Appaloosa mare.

She stands content, in her stall
with her newborn foal.
But... all movement thickens to slow.
Can strangers understand this fear,
of chilling her, in this 20-below weather
of my soul?

Death has walked so close.
I clean you off, a ritual,
this rinsing of a mother's hooves, legs.
New life stalks me as I work,
the foal nuzzling my ear, my neck.

He has so much to learn
in this first day of life.
I stroke his newborn's goatee,
dubbing him "Chris" Kringle,
born on December 28th.

God has blessed my life with dams,
and foals.
Would I have survived intact
without these four-leggeds
depending on me for food, water,
warmth?

Eleven months and a week
have gone by since we lost you.
You blazed your path
before your parents' time.
Now my horses comfort me
with their needs and noses.

Indian Removal Cartography

It's an old map, looks hand-drawn.
Starting in Georgia,
North Carolina, Tennessee, Alabama,
a broad swath of territory
belonging to the Cherokee,
yet shrunken so
from where the first Europeans found them,
that kidney-shaped province
splayed across the states
contracts down to these thin lines
marking the paths they were forced to travel.

This old-looking map
has been modified for the modern scholar
with gray-banded place names highlighted.
When you hover a computer mouse
over one of these shaded names,
pertinent facts appear.
From New Echota, capital of the Cherokee Nation
in 1838, now a state park,
to Fort Butler, one of five North Carolina stockades
where Cherokee were held under foul conditions,
to Fort Payne, yet another removal fort and internment camp in
    Alabama,
to Ross's Landing where more than 2,000 were held prisoner
and departed in three large groups
to travel to Indian Territory by water.
The Unicoi Turnpike, an ancient war and trading path,
took other groups onto the Trail of Tears,
is now designated a Millennium Trail.
Charleston, Tennessee, where 13,000 were held
for months, waiting to begin their unwilling trek
across five states in winter.

Hopkinsville, Kentucky,
Chief Whitepath died and was buried here,
remarkable for being one of the few
whose graves are known.
Hover long enough over Hopkinsville
and the screen will tell you
"Most of the thousands of Cherokees who died on the Trail
    lie in unmarked graves."

Crone

Sometimes I catch a glimpse of her
In the corner of my eye
As I pass the mirror in the hall
Or a storefront window
When the light is just right.

She is an older woman
Eyelids droop over her lashes
Like hoods on a game bird
Crows feet at the corner of each eye
Neck like a turkey gobbler.

Wisps of gray hair here and there.
Who is she? Why is she following me?
She resembles my mother,
Can't be, she died years ago.
Strange old hag cackles in my ear.

Dance by the Light of the Moon

My dark heart is heavy
With old loves
Littered with remnants of
Tattered refuse
I refuse to throw away
Clinging to every scrap of kiss
Every fragment of embrace
A half-eaten box of chocolates
In a red satin heart

All this clutter leaves
Little room for new loves
There's no place over there
Behind that icon of Adonis
Where I sit and sulk
In my dark heart
A place where I crush
The dried petals of roses
In my palm to see
If there's some fragrance
Left in them
I close my eyes
Grasp my knees
Try to will all the old love
Back to life
See the sparkle in those eyes
One more time
Bring the lilt back
In those steps
Wind up the music
For a spin
Around the room
With this one
Or that one
But
The music sounds like
Grandma's old Victrola
Never quite getting
Up to speed
Gonna dance with
The dolly with a
Hole in her stockin'
Knees keep a-knockin'
While she keeps a-rockin'

Crows

We passed the winter
Together
Hunkered down against
The snow
Cold wind biting between
Our shoulder blades
We said not a word
Of comfort or complaint
Only kept our thoughts
On spring
The warm sun
The fat worms

from The King of Kings County

When I was a kid, my father took me every fall to watch the Bowen family switch on the holiday lights at their Campanile shopping center. This was a big-time spectacle for Kansas City, and in preparation, they covered a grandstand with flag bunting and towed it out onto a bridge named for John Wornall, a slaveholder who'd owned a brick mansion just up the hill. My father claimed that John Wornall's whole importance stemmed from the fact that his was the only old-time house the Bowens hadn't demolished yet, but history didn't seem to matter much on Thanksgiving night as the shops closed down, the police barricaded off the streets, and the crowds poured into the Campanile. Then he was a great American, and we revered him, and that grandstand was set up where his bridge crossed Brush Creek and intersected with Bowen Boulevard, which made for a symbolic joining of great Kansas City names.

It would be hard to overestimate the crush of this great event. To get out on the bridge you needed a ticket, which, as an "associate" of the Bowen Company, my father wore clipped to his hatband. He also made reservations at the Campanile Steak House six months in advance. My mother was a southerner and disliked the cold, so we lingered over our creamed spinach and prime rib, watching TV crews unload cameras the size of freezers (I'm talking the early sixties here), and planes buzz overhead, until my father wiped his mustache and said, "Let's get in the thick of it." He knew something about the thick. He went about 260 in those days, one of those formerly athletic men whose size allowed dandifications that others might not risk. He had long, white-blond hair, he affected foulards and straw boaters long after they were out of date; he could be observed in tan seersucker and white oxfords in the spring—a hell of a wardrobe, which embarrassed me greatly. But his favorite outfit was a yellow suit of baggy linen with a black string tie and a kid gray fedora. Following him in that getup, as he elbowed his way down Bowen Boulevard that cold November night, his hair all glittery gold against his neck, was like following a crazed Custer through a welter of black-hatted braves.

And what a crowd it was. I didn't give a damn about any of it. Once we'd showed our ticket and gotten mother, who was short, to a place where she could see, all I cared about was looking at Geanie Bowen, Prudential's granddaughter, who'd be sitting on the stand. I knew she was in pain. We'd seen the whole Bowen clan out there at five o'clock when we drove to the steakhouse, already screwed down into their folding chairs with nobody around except for a few members of the Ladies' Auxiliary stapling up the bunting. By now, Geanie's lips were green—she was a skinny girl, a red-head—and she had secretly slipped her arms inside her dress. Being skinny myself, I assumed a sympathy between us. The creek that we stood over, for instance, had a concrete floor and grassy banks but in its ice-rimmed trickle, toilet paper flags and turds floated past. I knew that Geanie felt the same contempt that I did for the woolen-coated crowd who stood down there in their own mess, cheering her family.

Nobody else recognized these incongruities. Or rather, my father did, but he thought they were great. I saw his eyes get swoony when Prudential Bowen stepped up to the podium. He both loved and hated the old bird. "How the hell can you imagine that," he'd say afterward to my mother, loud enough that I could hear it in my room. "That crinkly bastard getting thirty thousand people to come out and clap for him in a hay field. It's like Khrushchev reviewing troops. Not a single ounce of charisma but he's got all the strings tied up backstage." He always said these parts about craftiness or cheating loudly, so I could hear. My interest in rectitude was a worry to him constantly. "You know why Brush Creek stinks, don't you?" he had more than once asked me. "Because Prudential bought all the land along it upstream, then told the city if they wanted to run their sewers to it, they'd have to build him a system too, for free. Think of that: free sewers, and then you just float all your crap out and back to the city. That's how a real businessman does it." It was important, in his eyes, that I know such things.

160

The Cannon Ball

Flash floods at dawn, rivers red with clay;
By noon a cracking sun, wind rasping my bones.
Behind me Gettysburg, the black muskets
Splintered, Brother James stiffened by rumor,
His only grave in my unsodded mind.
I carry death inside my saddlebags;
Its heaviness thumps the flanks of my sweating bay;
I feel its iron roughness in my bones.
We rode together, Brother, stalwart as muskets,
Ready as boys tracking a lusty rumor
Through the tall grass. Oh, what fool's gold we mined,
Wrapped in the glitter of spring! Our bravest flags
Rot now in the fields of Gettysburg where muskets
Rust beside the helter-skelter bones
Wrenched from their springs, and I hear a bodiless rumor
Walking the groves, whimpering like the wind.
My legs are stiff in the stirrups as twin muskets,
For I carry you in the litter of my bones,
James, the cannon ball pressing my side like a tumor.
But I will plant it soon, at sundown salute it with muskets,
A new grave in a land without old stones.
And if a dark truth grows, these hands will husk it.

The Forecast

Perhaps our age has driven us indoors.
We sprawl in the semi-darkness, dreaming sometimes
Of a vague world spinning in the wind.
But we have snapped our locks, pulled down our shades,
Taken all precautions. We shall not be disturbed.
If the earth shakes, it will be on a screen;
And if the prairie wind spills down our streets
And covers us with leaves, the weatherman will tell us.

Menorah Hospital, May 30, 1971, 9:55 a.m.

Anna Gabrielle,
    your mama, holding her breath,
    shoved you out into the morning
    with four stunning pushes
    her smile an arc of sunlight
    splashing my face
    as you cried hello to the already world.
    Then she called out softly:
    My grandmother died in this hospital.
    Her name was Anna
        and I loved her.
    But, Death,
        now I'm even.

Dirty Song

Crime drifts like water vapor through the air,
through exhausted lungs, like CO_2.
We breathe it in, almost unaware.

We cough it up, like a TB patient's prayer.
Always it offends our lives anew,
drifting like water vapor through the air.

Always we blame the others for what's there,
for the detritus from which the fungus grew,
for poverty blossoming almost everywhere.

We celebrate the ritual called despair:
a mixture of palaver, promises, mortgages due,
corruption drifting like acid through the air.

Your bus is leaving. You think you've got the fare.
A robust voice assures you that it's true.
But your pockets empty as you climb the stair.

You cry out. You're in the spotlight's glare
for one bare moment, then the fare is due,
and unwanted as crime you're drifting through the air.

Looking for the Foreman

Over their shoulders
the workmen look for the foreman,
for his black car touring the site.
Between truckloads of earth and rock
they lounge in a paradise of shade,
sip from thermoses and bottles
stashed by the side of the road.

All day they carry the sun on their backs,
deflect it with hats, look down into their shadows
as if into deep lakes of themselves.
Between scoops they lean on shovels.
Brick by brick, board by board,
their work collects slowly, a labor
of seasons, a long history
of burdens and hammers,
of many measures, of hauling
and shoving, of waiting
for something to fit,
something to fall.

When done is done,
they collect their checks,
dream of some big payoff
far from the job.

_DAVID OWEN

from **The Dime Store Floor**

I thought a lot about memorable odors recently, during a trip to Kansas City, where I grew up, because my sister, whose name is Anne, suggested that we visit a few places we remembered from our childhood, to find out whether they still smelled the same. Certain smells go all the way down to the core of memory, and encountering them again can set off reverberations. The first place she picked was one that had deep sensory links in both our brains: the medical building where our dentist's office used to be. The drinking water in Kansas City wasn't fluoridated until the nineteen-eighties, and when Anne and I were children cavities were so common that our dentist didn't make separate appointments for fillings: he went to work with his drill as soon as he'd finished digging the impacted Milk Duds and Jujyfruits from between our molars, and he worked so fast that the Novocain was usually taking full effect only as he was finishing up. The smell that Anne and I now found in the hallway outside what had once been his office was familiar — volatile solvents and fear? — but was disappointingly faint, except when an orthodontist's door opened as we passed and a woman and her grumpy teen-age daughter brought a gust of it with them as they exited. I hadn't been in that hallway for more than thirty years, but in all that time its appearance had scarcely changed, and as we snooped around I rediscovered many things I'd forgotten, such as the old-fashioned typeface of the gold-leaf lettering on the dark wooden office doors (although the names on the doors were different)....

The most enduring and evocative remembered smell from all our growing up, Anne and I decided, was the smell of the Nelson-Atkins Museum of Art, the objective of innumerable field trips. As we drove there, I could easily generate a mental simulacrum of its smell, a concentrated essence of antiquity, brass polish, school shoes, and institutional gravity. When I was three or four, my mother enrolled me in art classes in the museum's basement, and on the first day she led me down a marble hallway and into a room filled with children I didn't know. I remember the gray steel-and-Masonite stools we sat on, and the shallow tins of bubbly, earth-smelling red and green tempera paint, the first liquid paint I'd ever got to use. I was wearing corduroy overalls, and in the front of them my mother had cut a slit so that I could go to the bathroom without needing help with the straps—a clever innovation that, to me, was a source of embarrassment and dread. The hall outside the art room had a powerful smell—as powerful as the smell of a doctor's examination room—and that smell, I discovered during subsequent visits, was even stronger in other parts of the building and, especially, on the marble staircase outside the museum's auditorium, one flight up.

Yet once Anne and I were back inside the building we could find no trace. The smell was gone from the basement hallway, gone from the marble staircase, gone from the auditorium itself, gone, even, from the gallery containing my favorite exhibit, the one of tiny carved-ivory cages and food dishes for crickets, from China. The Nelson underwent a major renovation and expansion a few years ago, and the old smell must have perished during the construction, annihilated by wallboard compound and modern building codes. In one hallway—which now had an alien scent despite looking exactly as I remembered it—I put my nose close to the gap between a locked door and its jamb, thinking that I might be able to whiff a vestige in the closet behind it. But there was nothing. And, eerily, today I can no longer reproduce the old smell in my mind—as though my knowledge of its extinction at its source had scoured it from my memory.

The next place we tried was a store that was called the Dime Store when we were children. It went out of business a few years ago but has been revived, in the same space, as the (New) Dime Store, by two people we knew when we were growing up....

As Anne and I drove to the (New) Dime Store, I predicted that the building's interior atmosphere—which had once been flavored mainly by dust, plus a sort of comforting over-scent that was related to mildew in the same way that cognac is related to wine—would now be dominated by scented candles, and I was right. (Scented candle displays, in stores, are olfactory kudzu.) In addition, the old wooden floor had been cleaned and sealed, changing not only its smell but also the pitch and timbre of its creaking. Nevertheless, much about the (New) Dime Store seemed gratifyingly familiar. There was a broad selection of notions, just as there used to be, and the candy and toy sections looked very much the same, although the items had evolved. Most of the toys that I used to covet were things that, nowadays, are considered health or choking hazards, or potential causes of injury or blindness: cheap slingshots (made of coated wire); expensive slingshots (made of wood); BBs; Greenie Stik-M-Caps and hard-plastic projectiles called Shootin' Shells (for our Mattel Fanner-50s); red roll caps (for hitting with hammers — ideally, one full roll at a time, producing flame and plume of acrid smoke); a specific type of plastic pistol and its pea-like ammunition; and model cars and their intoxicating glue, which hadn't yet been reformulated to deter sniffing....

My Daughter, Her Boyfriend, My Poem

She writes
what she says
is not a poem,
is, instead,
about a poem
where he called
her a road
he wanted
to explore,
telling her
of girl roads
he'd cycled down before.

She tucks
thin books
of wise sayings
next to her compact;
from her window,
mountain mist's
sad like tears.
She knows, wants
me to know she knows,
alleyways
from country roads.

All this I've heard.
And anyone
who calls life
a road,
or thinks rain's
like tears
has a long way to go.
But, it's his cycle,
her window,
my poem.

August Letter

I'm water in a slow pond.
Algae holds the air.
You'd like it here—
time, trees, a chair in the shade.
Old turtle under the porch
sticks his neck out each June,
then sits down.
Blood ambles to the brain.
I could stretch back,
grow old like this.
You'd say, Look at that turtle
in the lawn chair—Look
at that wrinkled mud
where the pond's died.

PATRICIA CLEARY MILLER

Eleanor Elkins Widener Builds Her Library

Pietas, Gravitas, Virtus

Here my boy is safe. He smiles at me,
his finger in his book. He left these books
to me. They glow now, all warm morocco,
bright red, green, gold — no colors of the sea.

He smiles at me, *Nearer my God to thee*
nearer to COME UP COME UP he led us out,
pulled families up from steerage. While shouting
officers shot themselves, Captain Smith plunged clear.

This heater does not warm, our guard shivers,
yet silk draperies, velvet, safeguard Dickens,
Shakespeare, Stevenson: first editions. Harry
had Widener's eye for value, my money.

Oh, come ye back. No one dare change these stones.
He lives. Now he will know where to come home.

Harry Elkins Widener, along with his father, perished on the Titanic. In his memory, and fiercely with her own money, his mother built the Harvard University Library, decreeing that no stone be changed. The small Reading Room is kept as a shrine, with young Harry's own rare books.

Cassandra at the Café

Cassandra's at the bar forgetting Agamemnon,

No thought of the blue Aegean or the last sheep
Letting its throat go like red wine on the stone.
One sip and her teeth freeze in bas-relief against

Her tongue, saline as an oyster hiding its pearl,
What she knows bypassing domestic trouble
Easy as water over the mind's stubborn altar.

Foreknowledge is a tendoned hand binding
The sacrificial body to the fact she'd wash away
In libations of tequila and scotch, flushing

Wild animal fear from the animated brain
That despite intention names moment and loss —
Brass tacks of memory nailing her prophetic palms

To a cross that stands straight in muddy ground
She doesn't think able to hold root, or voice future.
Who wouldn't choose cool comfort, past and present

Nested finally quiet in the heart? Cassandra
Would rather live in denial, drink the fisted grip
Of imminent fate down until the blessed entrails

Are ordered for good on the unbiased pillar
Of her spine, the sapling meant for kindling
Moist enough to keep its green and thwart fire.

Portrait of Jaleania

Her hands were more knotted at the knuckles
than 15 years should know, fingers too swollen
for the boyfriend to put a ring on.
She watched him in the halls at school
hold other hands, smaller hands
which ask less of him. Her legs swelled, too,
from carrying his son while waiting tables,
filling ketchup bottles, wiping the floors down
" 'til way past closing." I went to her home,
to take her to a poetry reading. I waited
in the front room while she left to get her coat.
A fast food dinner spilled fries and Hot Wings
on the sofa, and a stained coffee table held
her Physics book, face down, wings open.
Next to it, a greasy *Crime and Punishment*
paperback, I assigned for class, opened
to the trial part where Raskolnikov asked the same
question she had about who gets punished.

Performing the High Wire

Before Easter a teacher sent you to the office
where the lady from the Children's Fund
presented you with a brown package of clothes.

Walking back to the classroom, you hid
the embarrassment of carrying your
New Start in a meat wrapper. You learned early
that a joke at your own expense

put you in command of effacement. As class clown
you assumed a persona, the package like a chair
on the tip of your nose, tight roping an imaginary high wire
to your desk. You swayed above the eyes
of your classmates, teetering

like nothing mattered but the circus.

Denial

He seldom speaks of the war,
but he remembers—

From our dive bomber we watched
a fiery mid-air collision —
stopped breathing
when only the gunner bailed out,
plummeted to earth
like a bomb we'd dropped.
His parachute never opened.

We found his broken body,
buried it under a mound of dirt
in the Guadalcanal jungle,
stuck a propeller blade
in the ground for his monument,
marched back to our tent,
shot craps for his watch and socks.

On Sunday,

Dad drove us on hilly dirt roads to Grandma's house.
She said a prayer to save our souls,
used a kitchen chair for her walker,
served us chicken fried on her corn cob stove,
potatoes and tomatoes raised in her garden,
grape jelly made last month.
Her rule — no fun and games on Sunday,
just visit in the parlor, separated at the doorway
by a curtain of beads we dare not swish.

But Dad saddled up Old Tex for us to ride
so we'd ask to come back to Grandma's.

The Been-To

They expect him to return
with gifts, stories,
with shells and pretty rocks and feathers:
he brings nothing
but himself after all this time
as though back from some secret war,
not the man he was.

Why not? Something
about the eyes, a little more
distant, perhaps, though they were always
a bit too far away. He refuses
to answer questions, his words
as he always spoke them
but hollow, yes,
a little emptier.

His skin a little darker.
He came to the source
of the dark river and believed
he saw Kurtz
put his finger to his lip, say,
Tell nothing, nothing of what you saw.

As though he needed to be told.

It's Cool to be in India

A New Delhi student offers me
opium for my blue jeans.
He backs off as he reads
my thoughts, hamburgers and guilt.
A relief of Ganesa, the elephant-headed god,
reminds me of Dumbo and Disneyland.
A Muslim goes into a trance
mourning the death of Mohammed's grandsons;
the white of his eyes matches
the hospital walls, my bowels inflamed
with dysentery. "Hepatitis," the nurse
in a sari says, missing the vein
in my right arm with her needle.
She shakes her head as I write
my name. I am cursed for being
left handed in this country, squatting
over a hole for hours with a roll
of toilet paper by my feet. Beggars sleep
in front of movie posters with American
sex appeal. Women do a thousand dances
with their eyes. I hike in Nepal
with a school teacher from New Hampshire.
She holds her index finger in the air
and jogs up the hills. She says yoga
and Jane Fonda have kept her in shape.
Our Sherpa guides disappear with our packs.
We are food for tigers,
we shave our heads for Krishna.
K.R. Narayanan says I am a spy
for the CIA. I have built
my hut for monsoon season,
received ablutions in the Ganges.
I walk around in sandals,

no longer fear worms that drill through
the soles on my feet, work their way
up my veins. Daily, I tend
lingam shrines by sitting on them.
I renounce all possessions except
my gourd and my Walkman.
I marry a water buffalo;
he helps me with my rice crop,
is nicer than men.
He tells me he wants to see California,
be on the cover of *National Geographic*.
I don't make him any promises.

On Line at the Post Office

All that is needed is that a state of war should exist.
—George Orwell, *1984*

The line stretched from the lobby doors to the "Wait Here" sign. People shuffled mail and watched traffic pass outside. One man chattered on a cell phone for everyone's benefit in cryptic, allusive phrases. Could have been business or personal. Hard to tell the difference anymore.

The woman who now stepped up to the counter was, I realized, sending a box to a soldier. After a year of sending packages to Iraq and another to Afghanistan, I knew the signs. The customs form in sextuplicate fluttered in one hand. Its dense print ominously warned of a possible phytosanitary inspection. The letters APO were scrawled awkwardly on her box. Fatigue and urgency had drained her face. Maybe I had a similar look. I felt instantly connected and found myself calculating whether I'd be done in time to catch up with her. The others in line faded away as if a fog had engulfed them.

My box contained soup, canned chili, power bars, beef jerky, vitamins, canned fruit, canned vegetables, canned tuna, tooth-brushes and floss, and magazines. Mostly food. My wife and I had read that MREs didn't provide enough calories for foot-soldiers in the mountains. And they tasted so bad that soldiers carried Tabasco sauce to make them edible. Or they'd mix bizarre combinations: dried creamer, instant cocoa, and crackers for S'mores. Pork and beans and jam? Here's a weird factoid: MREs are purposely short on fiber so soldiers don't get ambushed in the woods with their pants down.

Our son was somewhere in eastern Afghanistan, in the moun-tains that bordered Pakistan. I learned later that he was in the Korengal Valley, the so-called "Valley of Death"—a rugged land-scape of tangled trees and barren mountains I swooped through regularly on Google Earth, wondering where he was in the forests and slopes of my satellite view.

A postal clerk once told me that with delivery confirmation I could be sure my son received his package.

"In the Afghan mountains?" I asked, incredulous.

He assured me, yes. I paid the extra fee just to prove he was wrong but never bothered taking the unconfirmed receipt back to show him.

Few Americans have any personal stake in these wars.

Their mail probably has nothing to do with war.

Standing on line—there was always a line—I imagined other postal customers going off to their next errand in the thriving shopping plazas all around the post office, off to Home Depot, Wal-Mart, the video store, the car wash. Back in September 2001, our leaders told us to shop. Shopping would save us. Shopping was patriotic. We embraced this patriotism.

Sometimes people told me, and probably the lady at the counter, too, Thank him for his service. They were sincere; they meant well. But now, after years of war, and with so little sacrifice by so many and so much by so few, phrases like that resonate in the hollow white noise of bumper-sticker platitudes that have become the background chorus of our lives.

Our language has been damaged, our ability to express ourselves impaired by extremists, simplistic thinking, Swift-boating. By war. Perhaps such expressions are a distillation of sorts, all we can say as we stand bewildered in the rubble of chaos and distortions that have brought us to this moment. Our ability to respond is failing. Language is failing.

War has become a natural force. We are at war in Afghanistan, but not against Afghanistan, at war in Iraq, but not against Iraq. We're at war against terror, which is neither a state nor a country nor a people. We live in an Orwellian nightmare in which war exists for its own sake, or to provide some warped sense of stability, or to preserve power for the powerful.

The strategy of war gets more debate than its necessity. The case for war has been made—for generational war, for endless war. That we should always be at war is settled. Our policy is to make war.

By the time I reached the parking lot, the woman at the counter was gone. I would have liked to say hello, perhaps find out where her package was going.

But I just headed home, where I tacked the customs receipt on my bulletin board along with dozens of others.

Camping in the Stull Cemetery

We join hands and form a circle,
letting the fire crack until blue.
Standing together in the timothy,
we suddenly burst into dance.
Intensely loving one another,
we roll in the weeds and pick
cocklebur from our backs.

Then we remember why we live.
And that becomes our coin.
Lying all night by dark woods,
framed in the moon's old slurry,
wrapped in the crazy quilt
of modern life, we drink
the wine until it's gone.

And no one sulks about the end
of the world, wars and rumors
of war, apocalyptic horsemen,
driverless cars, heads rolling free.
We've had enough of angst.
Lying close to the fire we hear
the June-bugs pop.

Late In the Day

Not much happens, really.
I've sat by the window a long
time, watching the river birch
do absolutely nothing but
stand in the same old place.
The ragged peel of the bark,
no different than yesterday,
hangs loose for the show.

Thing is I rather like the tree
we planted as a sapling, thin,
delicate, apt to die at first frost.
And you'd think to look at it,
as it rose and spread the limbs,
that death was imminent.
But through the years several
branches sheltered the birds .

I gaze out the window and
ponder the next few lines.
A squirrel pads across the roof.
The roses look a bit ragged
after last night's hailstorm.
The coffee I savor will cool
in the cup, losing its charm,
and I will rise and meander

to the kitchen, pour another
cup, return to the computer,
and revise my muse to fit
the aging of the day, from
dawn crying in her diapers
to mid-afternoon, and me
wedged in this languid hour,
when words fly blind.

Stark Weather

> . . . and it seem as though i could
> see ny heart before ny eyes, turning
> dark black with Hate of Rages, or
> harhequinade, stripped from that munner
> life leaving only naked being-Hate.
>   -- Charles Starkweather

On the Great Plains in March
the wind blows for days.
Gutter pipes vibrate, shingles flap;
things begin to come loose.
Once they found old Miss Purdy
wandering at midnight on U.S. 40,
her nightgown billowing
over her spindly, blue-gray thighs.
It took three deputies to hold her down
till the doctor arrived.

On the Great Plains in March
the dry elm scrapes
at an upstairs window,
dust devils swirl and disperse
across the wide, empty fields,
and a pistol shot sounds
no louder that a screen door
slapping on a porch.

My Father's Laugh

It was a bursting, like when the cap
comes off a boiling radiator. He'd buckle
and turn red; big tears would runnel
down his cheeks, drip off his nose.

It took tits to bring it on, bazooms,
or idiots or feet doing their stuff
or a drunk taking a cross-eyed fall
into a six-tiered wedding cake.

It took Red Skelton or Jerry Lewis
or me one day with my new-bought
Whoopee Cushion, making blats
and peeps for him, tootles and flaps.

He couldn't stop till I did, a turnaround
from the times he'd catch me in his sights,
finger jabbing home those points
about straightening up and flying right.

I was bursting too, his begotten son,
his Siamese twin, busting a gut,
he'd say, laughing my ass off — the two of us
funny as a rubber crutch.

Kong Bares His Soul Regarding
Miss Tyrannasaura Regina

OK, so we're not the perfect royal couple,
me a hermit and her temperamental
as a hot volcano and not what you'd call
"pretty." Standoffish, too, as if

warm blood and opposable thumbs were too
lowbrow for dining out on stegosaurus
guts. Maybe I could wear my hair
shorter, get a tail piece, learn to hiss
and bolt my food. Maybe then I'd find
the nerve to crush her boyfriend's spine
and ask her out.
                    I should know better, but
Those eyes, so green and deep you hardly
notice her head is two-thirds teeth
and her toenails lay down sets of foot-deep
divots.
          I don't know. Last night
I dreamed of someone lovelier: swept in
from the sea, golden-tufted like a bird of paradise,
who needed rescuing from pterodactyls
and teeny-weeny white men, and sang to Kong
in a voice so high it broke his heart.

Fool Noir

It felt like every other night in this crummy town,
like you'd been cold-cocked and stuffed in a dumpster,
like when a pet store ferret crawls up your pant leg
and bites you in the balls, like when you've sloshed in
wet cement and don't know it till you see the tracks
on your new carpet, yeah, and then see darker tracks,
from when you set your sock on fire trying to light
a cigarette the way Bogie did in *The Maltese Falcon*
and danced hitch-kick flambé around the living room,
knocking Dad's ashes off the mantle and into the fondu
you put out for the big party nobody but the cops
showed up for. Yeah, business as usual in dullsville
—till *she* walked in, but that's another story. Yeah.

Silent running

Forty years ago I drove a yellow Studebaker, a friend on my hood.
One or two more clung to the roof, and inside five or six of us
      singing O roll your leg over . . . .
Two plumes of drying barf streaked away like painted flames from
      the two rear side windows.
A little print of Bruegel's Peasant Wedding hung from the clothes
      hook in back, to class up the act.

More than once Sundays 2 am-ish we would drive like this down the
      hill of Charbonnier Road
Until just the right speed, and then I'd cut the flathead engine, push
      in the clutch, and we'd coast
Powerless downhill in silence, and if in moonlight I'd cut the
      headlights
And we'd go in near-darkness, all of us quieted, until a driver
      coming towards us
Got within range, when I'd pull the headlights on and tweak the
      ignition key,
The engine backfiring like a twelve-gauge just as our fellow traveler
      passed by going uphill.

::

Today I am that fellow traveler jacklit by a beast half-young-man,
      half-Studebaker.
I am a flathead six-cylinder engine firing its coup de grâce,
      headlights giving myself the third degree.
The windows of the self rolled down, I am a blue eye in the ditch of
      Charbonnier Road, I am a pink ear,
And 2 am blows by, and a minute later, 2 am blows by, and a minute
      later, 2 am blows by,
So clearly I live now and then in Bruegel's peasant bride who herself
      keeps her eyes closed, clasped hands

Resting in her lap, the quiet everlasting being magnetizing the Babel
    of her own wedding.

::

And my friends? Jim lies spreadeagle, gripping the chrome winged
    hood ornament,
Bob and I reach out our windows, hold him by his ankles,
Triangulating him. Mike and Ron lie on the roof, grab on to the rain
    gutters,
Friends in back reaching out to hold them on by their legs.
All of us coast downhill towards the Missouri River bottomlands,
    each of us holding on to another,
Ignorant we would live forever, true, but in moonlight at most,
And without one word, save the wind's admonitions.

Greasy Joan

When roasted crabs hiss in the bowl,
Then nightly sings the staring owl,
To-who:
Tu-whit, tu-who! A merry note!
While greasy Joan doth keel the pot.
— William Shakespeare

As cold gains a tighter grip
and meals grow heartier,
Joan is in the kitchen
where she stews, bastes, and broils,
works up a sweat,
sets the feast on the table,
hops up to fetch the butter.
"More sauce!" "Too much pepper!"
"Tu-whit, tu-who," the family's ringing note.
"Dessert time and better be quick."
"Kickoff time approaches."
She clears the table, rinses dishes.
Her hands and arms grow scummy
as the kitchen sink, a greasy orange.
Her teeth are set on edge
as she scrapes knuckle bones into the trash
and garbage down the sink,
fends off the dogs,
clears the counter top of cats
while inside the living room
the family cheer or boo the plays,
some enthroned on the couch,
menials crouching on the floor.
Children whine. Their noses drip.
And in the kitchen Greasy Joan
keels the pots, hearkens to the owl's cry.

Sunday Sisters

They switch and sway in the church
with their hallelujahs and amens
in pink, yellow, red dresses
and big brim hats
each sitting up front
vying for the preacher's attention
while the organist plays an up tempo tune
to the choirs' stomp down version
of "Going to the river to be baptized."
As the trays are being passed,
the clinking of money sounds
like someone hit the jackpot.

The preacher rises to deliver his sermon,
all six feet and three inches of dark
chocolate wrapped in a tailored suit,
deep dimples and a devilish smirk
hypnotizing the Sunday sisters into
submission as they all
lean forward so he can
get a good look at them.
He scans the row of legs crossed
at the knees, some of them slightly gapped.
He asks the question, "Why are we here?"
From the front row a husky voice
moans, "To get some religion and
a little chunk of you on the side."

Swaggalicious

A natural swing, a flow of his arm
    a drag of his foot with a smooth move,
        groove scratching the concrete while
           stepping to a beat in his head.

      Whether in public or at home,
        the swag is stuck like skin, or
          hair that stands on end,
             when a cool wind blows.

       He doesn't even know he has the walk,
         it's a too hip for the room kinda' walk,
           he's humble but can keep it under control.

        His style is charismatic,
          as he blows your mind,

             but he can't deny his swaggalicious thang
               that cannot be copied
                  even if it was cloned.

How I Came to Love Jazz

— for Toni and Les

My mom and dad met
when she was 13, he, 16.
They lived in Brooklyn.
She was friends with his sister, Nell
and he became friends
with her brother, Jack.
Dad played the violin,
had to go past Sarah Vaughan
and her gang on his way
to lessons, and they'd chase
him 'cause he played the violin.
So he quit.
Uncle Jack introduced
dad to bebop.
It was still new then
and denounced as devil music:
Coltrane, Bird, Monk.
He couldn't understand it all,
but couldn't stop listening.
My mother was fair
with long, almost black hair.
Dad and friends used to
call her "snowy with blowy."
In those days,
my darker-skinned dad
couldn't pass
the brown paper bag rule,
but mother did not care about that.
She took dance lessons from
Lena Horne, just a young girl in
the neighborhood making a living.

Aunt Nell took classes
from Katherine Dunham.
Mom's friend dated Harry Belafonte,
but she married someone else.
Dad took my mother to Coney Island
and jazz clubs, where she drank only milk,
and he taught her about jazz
and how to smoke cigarettes.

The Other Side of Windows

*I little dreamed how much I'd give now, if I could,
for one scowl and a word of discouragement.* Carl Bettis

From under her full brimmed hat,
a bit of a smile, a sideways glance,
full of things that makes you wonder,
as when passing an almost closed window.
She's dressed in a wrap dress, chunky heels,
somewhere in Brooklyn, circa 1944.
Her son peers through the windshield
between the wiper swipes of driving rains
on his way eastward — home.
After the rains, the mist and clouds
look like smoke, like the earth
had been doused after a big fire.
Her time is passing now
in front of windows. He sits next
to her, flipping through decades of photos;
they stop at one of her in a wide brimmed hat.
He is talking in his loud voice,
trying to get a rise,
but she only smiles, is mostly silent,
watches squirrels, birds, shadows,
rustling leaves, his car passing by
when he goes. He tries to spot her
in her window but can't see in.

It's a Food Town

She says it has always been a blues town
even when it was a jazz town
but she's wrong it's a food town
because I can't choose between
costillas en chile verde up on Summit
or samosas piping hot on Lexington
scalding pho in the market
dumplings on 39th street
chicken spiedini on fifth
or gyros falafel and pizza at the curb
I don't want to argue Gates Bryants
Jackstack LC's Oklahoma Joe's
or your granddady's all night long
Italian and Austrian in the freight
peppercorns above the trains
peaches from the tree
or double cheese & grilled onions
on Broadway or Baltimore
taquitos on Central or Independence Avenues
greens in Eden's garden
strutting chickens north and south
pollos ricos shrimp biryani sashimi
roumalade ooh la la
mix the bunch and bring me
iced sweet tea and bourbon on the side

Retrato de Familia

Mi familia stands facing the camera
from mi abuela to mi prima Leonor

and tío Guillermo to mi tía Emerita
framing the line that hugs close to the wall
Us kids are entwined and woven into the legs
elbows and waists of assorted other tias and tios

We are a varying shades and tints
pink flushed cheeks next to olive brown arms
questioning ebony eyes beneath jet black curls
deep brown folds embracing plump peach cheeks

A bashful white face beneath golden braids grins
at mi primo Rafael's twisted face
as he succeeds in spoiling the decorum
of the family portrait

Then the stern look of mi abuelita
as she eyes the children that at any moment
threaten to spill across the polished floor
like a stew about to overflow the boiling pot
as if with one look she can hold us back
in the container in the very pan
that has stirred our different flavors
into this mix of savory creole mestizo moor
from the sands of Arabia and the broad stretch of Africa
and the spreading tubers of Andalus and Catalunya
and the indigenous migrants from the north
and the bridge to the ancestral lands
to the mother to the patria
to the folds of the Rift Valley

We simmer and the bubbles subside for an instant
until the hand with the camera gives a thumbs up
and then this stew spills across the floor
to the door to the streets to the city
to the hills to the sea
to the discomfort of those who fail to see
the varying tones and tints
of our rapidly growing family

Belinka wants to be my teacher

"A true revolutionary has to sacrifice everything for his cause…" He stops mid-sentence and eyes the grocery store open in the middle of the night. "Madre de Dios, look at that thing."

He taps the wheel and points to the parking lot.

"The comrades are hungry and we need to get some food."

Inside, Belinka scans the aisles like a scout and continues with his lesson.

"José, the thing that was wrong with Manuel is that he was an upper class bourgeois and he could never identify with the people. Don't get me wrong. Everyone loved him and believed in him, but when he was on the run he dressed in the same style as if he were walking down Parque Arauco on a Sunday afternoon. He could not even dress like the working class, and that disdain was palpable, though he did not mean it to be. Look at me and you are not going to think bourgeois."

I look at Belinka and I don't think bourgeois, not with his long hair and ridiculous mustache.

"Belinka, why do all revolutionaries have such ridiculous mustaches?"

"It hides the bad teeth, José. Revolution is the biggest cause of bad teeth in the world. The things I have given up for the cause pain me more than my molars. Come here, José, closer to the wall, walk over here. Where is the cheese, man?"

"There is a whole section over there dedicated to cheeses."

The tears swell in his eyes as we approach. "Madre de Dios, mira todo este queso. That is a lot of cheese."

Who knew that revolutionaries were such connoisseurs. He grabs packages and pushes his dirty fingernails through the plastic and holds them to his nose till they almost disappear into that ridiculous mustache.

"If I believed in heaven, José, I would think I was there."

He fondles an endless variety of cheeses and discards them all after cutting into the plastic wrapping and taking one good whiff. I am embarrassed and though he pulls me closer I try to look away and act like I don't know this man.

"You know, José, one of my biggest passions is wine but the penultimate one is cheese. You know why I don't like the Argentineans? They have Reggianito and Sardo, knock offs of Italian grating cheeses, but Chilenos, we have Panquehue and Chanco, kick the shit out of those flaky cheeses."

"You sound like a cheese snob, Belinka."

"José, cheese is a very important cultural identifier. Look at the French—they got cheese for every second of the day. Hell, you sneeze in France over a piece of cheese and you've created a national treasure."

"Belinka, I don't think this has anything to do with revolution."

"Damn you, José, don't you get it? Zapata—tortilla and beans but damn better with cheese. Castro, Cienfuegos, Che—black beans and cheese, same for Sandino and Marti. What about the first commune? They had cheese all the way to the Bolsheviks. José, all over the world no army marches without cheese, no country fights without cheese. La Pasionaria yelled 'No pasarán!' with a big slice of Manchego in her mouth. Your revolution? Cheese, which makes this so sad to see. What cheese has your revolution given the world? Cheese Wiz, American cheese, yellow cheese, cheetos. No, José, give me a rancid French Roquefort so strong it makes you want to cry and throw up and I am in heaven. You know the upper classes ate that cheese but it belonged to all. It's peasant food. Come on let's go. I am getting hungry."

He turns and heads out the door without buying anything. In the car, on the way home, he picks up on the lesson.

"A clandestine movement must have strict discipline. In a revolutionary condition every fighter must control his basest impulses."

While he talks, his hands pull packages of cheese from the pockets of his coat: camemberts, cheddars, Swiss gouda, soft cheeses, smelly cheeses and then single-packed packages of American cheese, yellow cheese.

"Belinka, what gives with the bad stuff?"

"Like I said, José, in a clandestine movement every fighter must control his basest impulses. I abhor this cheese but we are broke and I could not afford to be choosy."

Witnessing
from *My Almost Certainly Real Imaginary Jesus*

In the Southwest Singles group, a disproportionately large number of us were secretly trying not to be gay. We went through the motions of dating each other properly, boy with girl and girl with boy, thus avoiding the risk of any real attraction. We witnessed as a recreational activity. Coming out of our sullen mouths, the gospel didn't sound like good news. Our "good news" emphasized hell. Not surprisingly, our efforts rarely bore fruit.

A group of twelve of us organized by Doug G. (the singles group had two Dougs) climbed into his mother's station wagon and headed for the American Royal Parade in downtown Kansas City to pass out tracts. The parade is always in early November, and it always rains. No one wants a soggy piece of paper from socially awkward, wet people. Besides, people don't want to be distracted from pretending for their children's sake that they are having a good time at the parade.

I wouldn't even have wanted one of the hackneyed tracts I peddled, and I supposedly believed what it said. In a grotesque rendering of rough-looking people printed in the pamphlet, a gang war developed, and someone got stabbed. Right at the last possible minute before they bled to death, several characters, whom the reader had neither the time nor motivation to develop a concern for, got saved. I extended my copy half-heartedly to mothers pushing their strollers in wide arcs around me. The long-unaccepted tract went limp; I may as well have offered a bit of soggy toilet paper.

When I finally acknowledged that I was being a nuisance, I wandered out of sight of my group, apologized to the trees the tracts had been made from, and threw them into a trashcan. I found an empty spot on the wet sidewalk and crouched down to watch. Clydesdales, sheep, ponies pulling carts jingling with bells, goats, hogs, stallions, and mares all splashed toward the American Royal building where they would spend the next two weeks either waiting to perform or to be herded onto a truck for slaughter. A clown with a sad face tossed me a Tootsie Roll. It fell into a puddle, but I unwrapped and ate it anyway. Out of the corner of my eye, I watched for my evangelism team's energy to wane. When it did, we all filed back to the station wagon and rode for a long while engulfed by silence and the smell of wet hair and wool. A single new to our group finally spoke, "Don't you think that was wrong?"

"Wrong?" said Doug G. into the rearview mirror.

"What we did, bothering people, handing out cheap, badly written pieces of . . . . I mean, Jesus is more important than this, don't you think? We don't know a thing about the people we handed them to. What if someone they loved had just died? What if they have had such a hard time in life, they don't see how Jesus could love them? What if we were just bugging them while they tried to watch the parade?"

The beauty of tracts was that they prevented you from having to interact with the unsaved. They worked just as well to wash the blood of the unsaved from your hands as did talking to someone and taking the risk he or she would ask a question you couldn't answer.

"Don't you think Jesus bothered people?" Doug G. said. He had paid good money for the tracts.

"Well, yes, of course, what he said bothered some — made them think — but they came to him. He didn't follow them around shoving cheap little. . ." and he shook a wet tract, flinging water all over the singles in the first two seats. "He would have talked to them. He would have listened to them."

"You think they'll care about a parade when they're in hell?" Doug G. said. Everything was clear to Doug G.

"You know what I think? I think Jesus would have watched the parade with them. And he would have arranged to meet with them later. He would have tried to establish a rapport."

"A what?" Doug G. said, eyebrow raised.

Old Highway 9

The old man leans against his spade,
handle digging at the buckle on his overalls,
the clay-streaked forehead facing west
where reason dims: an orange flower
growing wild in the field that lights his face.
He holds a dozen rose rocks filched
near the red dirt road his grandchildren
call "Jesus Alley" and behind him the farmhouse
slumps in a coma of brittle scrub oak and shade.

A Conoco sign competes patiently,
the gas pumps shoulder their watch,
the glow fades.
And then the veil ignites his heart.
He will plant the stones now
in rows along the highway,
his body humming through the dark.

The Previous Owner

Our first house came with
his old hat, left hanging on a nail
placed for this purpose
just inside the garage door.
I bet it was his driving
or going out walking hat.
We'd heard he'd been taken to a home,
so perhaps he wasn't aware enough
to remind them to get it for him
the last time he left.
We figured out eventually
that he'd rigged the garage door
to flip a switch igniting a
Christmas tree bulb framed in
its own light plate on the bedroom wall,
probably so she would stop asking
if he'd remembered to shut it.
The neighbors shared he'd built
their brick walkway as well as ours
and the electrician kept saying
things were "interesting" and
he'd "never seen that before"
as he inspected the house.
So we left his hat
hanging in our garage
right where he'd carefully hung it.

The Silver Coin

The cows once believed that if you stand in a pond
shaped like a circle
during the full moon
you'll die. That was everyone's first summer
and it finally got so hot
the animals decided to hire another cow
to go in the water. Just to be sure.
This was a cow nobody cared much about
from the dry farm next door.
She squeezed through the wires one evening
saying there was no need for pay —
death would be enough.

She stood in the pond all night.

Now, during a full moon, the pond fills with animals
waiting for death. They call their pleasure
the other side of the silver coin.

Picture At Impact

It is 1855 and
two women are embracing —
their arms around each other's
bare shoulders. If you haven't seen
French daguerreotypes, I will acquaint you.
One of these French girls
looks like me — caught
young and angry in the command
to hold still with another — while wanting
to move with her body, her breathing
no matter the world be watching

for the slightest stir
or beat of the heart. Only my wish
to present us immoveable in our embrace
overcomes my desire
to blur our bodies with motion.
So we appear serene
as one can be staring into another's eye.
Our photographer behind the camera —
warm in his frock coat
and collar — Stay still as death,
he whispers.
Unflinching, I hold her tighter.

The Bedroom Too Near the Church Bell in the Duomo

I understand your view
that you have no space
for me but the untenable,
the small room so close
to the bell tower that
I might be disturbed by God
speaking with such regularity,
and, so, unable to sleep, sit
hours at the window, looking
through the darkness of Barga
for the divine face, wondering at the way
distance from divinity insists
we call ourselves to thoughts of prayer,
nothing derivative
from one country to another
in the certainty of those summoned,
nothing derivative in the way
we translate time
in the strike of a bell.

The Deer Come Down

— for Edward Weismiller

Expecting any moment an apparition
of deer, brown amid the green haze
of April woods, while the sun swoons
lower through spangled branches
and even the flare of flowering redbud
starts to dim, I lean on the fence rail

thinking of poets we've lost, or are soon
to lose, those most alert to the turn
of a leaf, or a line, the lift
of wind or veil, the faint complaint
of elm limbs rubbing together, those
among us who sensed, without seeing,

the first of the deer descend, testing
the air, flicking their white tails.

Miss Subways

— for Lawrence Ferlinghetti

"Meet Miss Subways,"
you wrote the year
my father dragged a final breath
through the silent room.

I never met Miss Subways.
I was too busy
whispering, "Come *on*,
Dad, one more!" too busy being
fourteen, too busy carrying
a hole the size of Utah
in my skinny chest.

Then came the scattering
of ashes at Jones Beach,
and I was too busy
throwing gritty stuff
into the waves
against a stinging wind

to meet Miss Subways
riding the Times Square
Shuttle back and forth
at four in the morning, like you,
Larry, and your hipster pals
who were with it
when I was without.

Yet the day would come,
whether in time hip, or
in time square, when I would ride
those same racketing cars
all night with your poems
in my pocket, and on my knee
a trembling notebook
filled with unspeakable words
as I tunneled the dark,
searching for Miss Subways.

Rue des Halles

It is a see-through day, Parisian sun
burning through mist, women in summer white
(from where I sit sipping *une bière pression*)
suddenly nude as they cross against the light.

Hours I searched for the lewd house where I lost
what claim I had to innocence, a score
of lives ago. Now in its place this bistro,
farting motorbikes, and tourists galore.

Which *doesn't* explain the girl sipping wine
two tables away, one foot up on a chair,
or why a boy's heart wildly beats in mine
to see her white neck, and arms long and bare.

Bathsheba, or Upon Learning the Earth
Once Had Two Moons

She bathes behind tight lattice
Screen, her nude body a mother's
Nude body not the nubile fantasy
Depicted by history painters.

And it's better for its truth, which it
Holds confident in the quiet lap
Of sponge to nape of neck.

And his truth is best. That he saw her and
Became over full, that his heart leapt fast,
Escaping the line of kings and God's gravity.

The world was round, and he led her
Around and her two moons
Divided the loneliness.

The bird in Satan's dress came later,
Along with the rock he never threw and
The screen he never split, flapping its ruby
Wings in the dust beside the sea of salt.

Of Sound in North Carolina

Would the sun not filter down
Through the pine vault like church
Light, creeping and silent,
You would not hear the primal
Warble stuck in the throat

Of the confederate dead,
Or the scream of sinking ship
Off Hatteras. And the seagull
Clamor in the square wouldn't be the pitch
Of too contrasting sky, too blue.
Mountains less swollen belly
And more crag, and crackle,
Could be left easy, like philosophy.

Open the window
And let the rain come through. Let the moon
Find the flicker running from the wind
That comes round wet and green
With memory.

All can be forgotten on the drive
To the coast as the night evaporates
East of Durham, past half illuminated
Tobacco shacks and the road laid flat
Into sinking pine forest and horizon
Opens wide for the tattooed masses
On the boardwalk, and seafood dives
Offer cold beer and oysters in shell
With sea water. And my babbling
Heart will read you Russell Banks
On the Outer Banks, and sing of Kundera
Kundalini in the key of flower markets
In Rimini, slow food, and walks
Among the ruins, until you're word blind,
Left eyes a'bob at the tip of pirate kites,
Listening for kids as they dip
Through surf, appearing and disappearing,
Lithe as otters atop the sandy shelf, chattering,
Breathless.

Meeting Frida

On the military post mid-century, I could go to movies
for a nickel and when I was finished with that life,
or thought I was finished, it was fifteen cents and a quarter
for the three hour epics, *Spartacus, Lawrence of Arabia,
Around the World in Eighty Days*. During the week,
I walked the mile to the theater that was more a church
on a hill that rose up above an infinity of Kansas plains
off to the west, and on the opposite side of the parking lot
there was a church. In the darkness of the theater, after
black and white newsreels with their deep-throated commentaries
on the encroaching Red Menace, the French defeat
at Dien Bien Phu, sputnik in a threatening orbit over our heads,
a solitary Japanese soldier still ready to die defending the atoll
where he was abandoned a dozen years after another war
        was retired,
I would see myself deep in someone else's story,
the poorly translated spaghetti westerns, the Roman Legions
out of sync with the dubbed dialogue, as if their lips
were clubbing the words I heard, oh, but the skeleton army
sown from the scattered teeth of some dead gorgon,
jumping out of the earth, shields and swords raised,
didn't need words. Then the British comedies with their agile
humor, it was a life robed in the dark, a sacrament of flickering
light, and now, four decades later, the sky a cold steel,
the parking lot a lake of iced asphalt, scattered with small islands
of stunted trees, the mall rises like a castle
with parapets of glass, and a dozen movie screens
crowded into one corner, where I buy a ticket from
a young woman, who turns and shouts to someone
in the back, "I sold one," then turns back
to me, "I hope you like weird movies."
The theater manager steps out to meet me
to explain, "It's kind of an artsy movie."

I say I don't mind. "Yes, but she's
a communist and bisexual." Robed in
darkness, finally, we meet alone.

Shore Birds

The contortionist in white panties touches
her hands to the sand, backwards, pelvis
thrust upward and out.

This is not a dream, as Magritte might
have put it, or maybe it is just one
wanderer's waking, impossible dream.

It could be a Federico Fellini dream, but
he would have cast a man
playing guitar into the scene

and a table with candles and a rabbi
holding a dreamlike white dove
above his flock.

That is not a dream either. The
guitarist sings, the sermon follows,
the challah torn and passed

and the dove white
as a contortionist's underwear,
as she stretches on the shore.

At a table perched above
the sand, we sip from
plastic chalices, Shabbas,

you say, as the faithful
murmur, as the dove ascends,
as the sun slips out from a cloud

and lacquers palm trees, hibiscus, with the last
blue light of day and paints a bright
white edge onto the gold and copper of your hair.

This is where the dream comes in. The song
and sermon make no sound in the breeze. All
we can hear is the chuffing

of waves, white-lipped jade, as they
cross-hatch toward shore.
OK, maybe not a dream,

or even a pipe, though that's what
I think of when you tug at my sleeve,
make me stop to inspect the bird

of paradise cantilevered in the crisp air
like a crane, not the bird (as the flower,
orange and blue and dewy in the sun, is neither

a bird nor a paradisal dream, piped into the senses)
but a blue steel crane, the kind that
spans air for heavy lifting,

the stuff we need to construct a
dream, say, this shabbas dream, however contorted,
like a ritualized handstand sprung on the sand.

O this shabby dream. If I could slap wings
like the white gull, if I could stretch the way
the woman on the beach

bends her limbs in prayer to the
rolling rhythms of the lake — then I would
share the dream: the rabbi's

silent sermon, the flock's silent prayer,
all of it a soundtrack to this shadow play.
Do you hear the guitar? The gull?

The waves? The turning of the earth
as the blessed moment slows? There is a prayer
here. A prayer, a blessing, a song, a winged dream.

Solo Flight

It was all approved by my instructor. I was going on the solo cross country flight required for a private pilot license. The course was triangular with one leg at least 100 miles long. I planned to start in Montgomery County, Maryland, land in Reading, Pennsylvania, and do the required three full stop landings. From there, the course continued to Salisbury, Maryland on the eastern shore of the Chesapeake Bay. I started early, so I could get back in time to relieve the babysitter.

The first leg to Reading was uneventful. Or as uneventful as possible when flying alone, thousands of feet above the ground, in a small Cessna with minimum instrumentation. I had to keep track of landmarks on chart and ground, while I scanned the instruments for malfunction warnings and the skies for other planes. All the while I was looking for pastures and golf courses that might make good emergency landing spots in case of engine failure. Everything was going according to plan. Just another day in the lab.

But that changed suddenly. I found Reading, but it did not look like a lazy airport. It was covered with planes. Small planes. Thousands of them.

And the tower was talking to multiple planes in the pattern. "Where do you...er...want me to land...which...runway?" I asked. He interrupted, "You a student?" "Affirma—ative," I croaked.

After what seemed like hours, I finally set the plane down. As I turned into the nearest taxiway, a small jet whizzed a few feet above the runway behind me. The plane shuddered from its turbulence. A guy with a flag waved me toward a place on the grass, in a long row of small planes. I hesitated.

Still clueless, I radioed the tower and said, "I would like to...er... do some take offs...landings." "You have to either stay or go," he said. "But I need take offs and landings," I said, a desperate tone in my voice.

"Stay or go!" he repeated.

"Okay, er...affirmative," I mumbled, and turned into the parking spot.

I shut the engine down, and stumbled out of the plane over to a woman taking fuel orders. Clutching my log book, I asked her to sign me off.

She burst out laughing. "A student on a cross country flight? You've got to be kidding!" She could hardly breathe she was laughing so hard. Gasping, she said, "Don't you know you are in the middle of the Reading Air Show?"

When I heard this, I panicked. I had heard about this air show. It attracts hundreds, thousands of planes, goes on for three days. Jets, parachute jumpers, wingwalkers, and military fly-bys. People fly in from all over the country just to watch it. Clouds of planes put on the show. I was lucky to land at all.

But here I was on the ground. Nothing bad had happened. Unbelievable. If I could do that, the rest of the trip would be a piece of cake.

I got back in the plane and started the engine. I called the tower and got taxi instructions. In front of me was a squadron of vintage planes. They took off in formation. I got my clearance and got out of there.

I landed at nearby Harrisburg, and the airport was nearly deserted. I did three landings, gassed up, and off to Salisbury I went.

The Chesapeake Bay was brilliant in the sun. The sailboats around Annapolis looked like a flock of birds. The bay bridge with its chronic line-up of crawling cars seemed like a toy.

The airplane hummed along, all indicators green. A few cumulus clouds kept me company. I was alone, self-reliant, invincible. Like a sailor crossing the Atlantic, solo.

I floated high above the rush hour traffic. I entered the crowded Montgomery County pattern, calm as if driving to the mall.

When I got home, my eight month old twins were oblivious to where their mother had been.

Kitt Peak Observatory

A mountaintop of telescopes in the desert
hovering above an ancient ocean floor.
The four meter sparkles in the sun.
We walk past signs that say
"Quiet please, day sleepers,"
for astronomers collect their stars by night.
The best part for me was searching space.
The best part for you was my breath
on your hand as you held it to my face
to shield my eyes from the blazing sun.

Accidental Angel

My uncle was paranoid schizophrenic and my babysitter. He made me my oatmeal and ovaltine, gave me my cod liver oil.

Winter times we went sledding, me clinging to his back as we sped down the hill, across the trolley tracks, down to the sea.

Summer times we walked the beach overturning stones. He taught me to skim the smooth, flat ones and to count—one-one thousand, two-one thousand, three-one thousand—so I could cock my finger just right to make the lighthouse flash.

His voices were no more mysterious to me than the radio voice of Gabriel Heatter with his More Bad News Tonight.

When he was distracted, I would ask, "What are they saying, Uncle?"

Sometimes he would shake his head and come right back. Other times he would say, "That I'm a worthless piece of shit."

That made my preschool self very angry. "Tell them they are wrong!" I'd say. "Tell them to go away!"

My uncle's hand would reach out and touch my cheek. His eyes were love-filled in a way I did not understand but liked. Later the eyes of men recently in love with me looked at me a little like that, but only a little.

When I was eight, he was "put away." I never saw him again.

Each Christmas he sent me a Betsy-Wetsy Doll and a silver dollar. For him I never changed. I still have his last silver dollar.

Later I went into a "helping profession," did the best I could with varying degrees of success.

Now I think my uncle was my finest moment.

Requiem for a Prodigal Daughter

She went on a protest march inside her head,
juggled arguments,
pretended to be a clay mug
when she was Haviland,
made us warm, filled
whenever she smiled —
but kept spilling out,
losing parts of herself.

The brilliant cut of her mind
grew cloudy.
She buttoned her old wool coat
against two decades of Minnesota winter.
January,
she could not brave another morning.

I like to think she was composing letters
to cheer us
when she fell asleep.

Left empty envelopes behind,
no forwarding address.

Her Dress

On a young summer morning
in the last honey of sleep,
I lie waking to the first sounds
in the big white house.

The floors creak and if I
stay in the shape of the last dream,
I can see my mother's dress
sway as she starts a fire, a meal.

I think her dress was woven
by the wheel of someone
living under the front porch.
She is in charge of beginnings.
I lie still
so not to miss a sound.

Eternal People

Often the smaller paintings hold them
as they stand in coarse muslin
and old shoes near a bowl of fruit.

They bear the look of those accustomed
to sun, to the purpose of the day,
and the eyes hold you

in a spell of constancy, a fullness ripe
as pears in the bowl, the dim lit room.

If you look away they will go back
to what they were doing.

Now and Zen

> *That miserable patch of events. That mélange of nothing while you*
> *were looking ahead for something to happen? That was it! That*
> *was life! You lived it!* —Clifford Odets

I have never learned to sew.

Go ahead and add that to my "bucket list" of skills I would like
to learn before I die. It used to be a long list; I once thought I might
like to know how to change the oil in my car or make jelly or *really*
know how to use a camera. But then, one day, you have an epiphany
and realize—or at least I did—that it's too late to take a class or sit
down with an instruction booklet. Not that you couldn't do it, but
that you don't give a damn about any of those things. That's the
moment when ennui trumps desire.

My friend Michael told me, shortly before his death in 1988, that
he had reached something close to a zen state when he gave up
caring about things anymore. He was living, if you can call it that, in
the spare bedroom of his mother's house, waiting to die of an AIDS-
related opportunistic illness. There were so many of those illnesses
knocking on his door by that point—he weighed 100 pounds and
had lost the ability to walk—that it was just a question of which one
would provide the fatal push, the final indignity.

I sat with Michael in that spare bedroom one afternoon, several
months before he died. We smoked menthol cigarettes together, one
after another, stubbing them out in a heavy glass ashtray on the
bedside table, cluttered with dozens of pill bottles and wadded-up
tissues and crinkly cellophane wrappers from the hard candy balls
that Michael sucked on all day, when he wasn't smoking.

Next to the glass jar of wrapped candies was a fat stack of
medical bills, held together with a rubber band.

"They'll never be paid," Michael said, pointing to the stack with
his long cigarette. "I'll die without life insurance, without health
insurance, without a dime. It bothered me for the longest time. And
then it didn't."

His bravado of a few years earlier — "I'm going to fight this thing and I'm going to win," he said. "People are beating this virus. I met a man who drinks a little bit of hydrogen peroxide every day. It kills the HIV virus, that's a known fact. You're not supposed to drink it, but he does and he says he feels a little better every day" — was gone. He had, he said, let go of everything in his new zen state. Even the will to fight.

"There's a theory, you know, that the right-wing fundamentalists and the Pentagon secretly hired scientists to create the HIV virus," he said, pulling another cigarette out of the silvery paper package. "The whole gay liberation thing of the 1970s was so disturbing to them, they wanted the gay community dead. So they found a way to do it. It's the modern version of the Holocaust."

Michael had many theories about AIDS. Sometimes he would call me in the middle of the night to elaborate on something horrible and new he had heard on television or the radio. "The government was actually *paying* infected men to go to the bathhouses and spread the disease," he told me once. "The better-looking guys got more money, of course."

I started laughing and after a sullen pause, he did too. I was afraid he might lose his sense of humor in his new zen state, but there were unexpected flashes of it from time to time. But the jokes became darker and darker.

He found great, grim hilarity in the story of a mutual friend — once terribly handsome and outrageously promiscuous back when both of those things counted for something — who had decided he could fend off the plague by marrying a nice Christian girl. He swore off his old wild life and made a kind of pact with God to follow the straight-and-narrow way. But two days before his wedding, he was arrested in a notorious cruising park in Indianapolis. "He offered a blow job to an undercover cop! Can you believe it?" (The nice Christian lady married him anyway and lovingly nursed him through a very quick, very ugly AIDS-related death.)

Michael called death "the unwelcome guest," although I suspect he welcomed death when it finally arrived, his so-called life had become so miserable. "You don't want to know how awful," his mother told me after the funeral. "Like a horror movie."

That's the reason I refuse to see films about serial killers or psychotic murderers in hockey masks or gruesome aliens. I see no entertainment value where innocent people die ghastly deaths. Why would I watch something like that? I've lived it!

And then, one day, I bought fabric and needles and thread. Since no one seemed interested in making a panel in Michael's honor for the Names Quilt, I decided that I would. But since I really didn't know how to sew, it was an awkward project and my fingers were scarred with needle pricks by the time I knotted the last stitch. The panel was accepted into the collection, but it didn't turn out as nicely as I had hoped.

"It looks like a loving grandmother made it," said my friend Jeff when we traveled to Washington D.C. in 1993, to see it as a tiny part of the giant quilt, unfurled, on the National Mall. "A loving grandmother with very severe arthritis."

I would like to make another quilt panel someday for another friend, Joe, who has yet to be honored. I've even bought the fabric and sketched out a few designs. But I can't bring myself to actually start the project. Is it fear or, even worse, am I slowly slipping into a zen state?

Ask me tomorrow.

Remember Me as a Writer, Not a Survivor

Feb 19, 2006 7:00 PM EST

My oncologist's nurse found out I was a writer. "You must keep a journal!" she said.

"I have nothing to say on this subject. I have *no comment*."

"But it could help other women."

"I don't care about them," I said.

That was true enough in the first few months after I discovered I had ovarian cancer, but what I didn't say was that writing had long ago lost its glow. I often found myself remembering Marcel Duchamp's last painting, "Tu m'" ("You Bore Me"). Even my work as a film critic for the local alternative paper suffered. I was often tempted to write, "Go see it and decide for yourself."

If typing, revising and mailing literary manuscripts was tedious before, it seemed absurd now. Statistics gave me a 30 percent chance of living five years.

Breast cancer's five-year survival rate is more than 80 percent, so it should not have surprised me when I thumbed through a list of local support groups and found plenty for breast and none for ovarian. Then it occurred to me: of course, they're all dead!

Not that death was a stranger. My poems tended toward death, death, death, pet death, death, sex, love, death.

Still, I was unprepared for just how unprepared I was to face my diagnosis. I would say it hit me like a train except that would describe the violence and not the despair, which was more like the embrace of a frozen corpse.

Ovarian cancer recurs frequently, and I could not shake the belief that no matter how well I'd done so far, I would not live long. Hoping for an edge, I asked the doctor about my cell type.

"Clear cell," she said.

"How does that affect my prognosis?"

"It doesn't," she said.

I soon learned she was a voice in the wilderness. Every

researcher on the planet, it seemed, thought clear cell the worst ovarian malignancy.

Panicked, I found an online group of "ovca sisters" and asked if they'd heard any good news about clear cell. In a word: nope. But they were glad I'd found them.

Every day I read messages from women who shared my limbo existence. Those of us in remission could imagine our futures in the grim posts of the ill.

Some members gave up good-paying jobs to become activists. Ah, civic duty. I just couldn't hear the call. However, I did have a standing invitation from the local paper to write on any subject. I suggested a personal essay in time for Ovarian Cancer Awareness Month.

The next day an editor phoned. "I hear you're writing a piece for us." "I already wrote it," I said. My productivity surprised even me. On Sept. 2, 2002, almost one year after my surgery, "Everything Changed" ran in *The Kansas City Star*. I got calls and letters.

I helped form a local support group, but I warned the members I was not a "group person." I might have only months to live, so I had to be choosy. Only one project really appealed to me. On the Internet I found cancer poems and asked friends to read them at an event, "Women, Interrupted: An Evening of Music and Poetry Dedicated to Cancer Survivors and Loved Ones Lost."

The event was a success but I wouldn't remain an activist long. Contrarian that I am, I started an argument.

The Pulitzer Prize-winning play "Wit," about an English professor dying of ovarian cancer, was, in my opinion, one long I-admire-your-bravery speech. So what if it put ovarian cancer on the map?

My ovca sisters were appalled. I was a traitor. But I was thinking like a writer again. I even wrote a new poem, titled "The Oncologist and Her Ghosts."

On the anniversary of my diagnosis, I followed the lead of another group member—I sent my oncologist a gift with a card that read, "Do you remember what you were doing three years ago today? I do. You were saving my life."

It was beginning to look like I would have to learn how to live again instead of how to die. I decided to apply to the Bread Loaf Writers' Conference in Vermont, where I had won a scholarship in 1989.

Bread Loaf required 10 poems, and I couldn't just trot out my sleek, muscular, published warhorses. I had to write new poems and quickly whip them into shape. It was a humbling experience, but I got the application in the mail.

My ovca sisters don't hear from me much anymore. They probably think I'm in denial, that I believe I'm cured. They couldn't be more wrong.

Cancer may take me yet—next month, next year or in 10 years. Whenever death comes, my obituary will not call me a cancer survivor. I will die, simply, a writer.

Dreams, Indexed

a found poem

Dreams of: architectural impossibilities, 57, 92, 121
of arriving at work in dressing gown, 89
of being told that Duke does not know one's surname, 121
of bull turning into a swan, 88
of card index in disarray, 137
of carrying analyst inside testicles, 80-82
of coins jammed in telephone, 81-82
of falling into machinery, 15, 101
of finding book containing truth, 124
of grating skin over salad, 81
of guest taking over kitchen, 95
of ink spots on suit, 89-90
of installing electricity, 92
of Iona Cathedral, 125
of joining exclusive club for visitors only, 124
of moon falling out of sky, 122
of nipples covered with squid ink, 81-82
of penises popping out of low-cut dress, 90
of sexual relations with detached female organ, 112
of ship bearing down on swimmer, 17
of sicknesses transformed into roses, 129
of swinging a cat, 75
of taking house to pieces brick by brick, 95
of word Earnest, 40

Yellow Jackets

My wife wonders
why nothing works.
Four times I've called.
Four times the man
has bombed, fogged, sprayed.

I keep telling him:
They built the nest
inside the walls.
Why should I have to tell him?
It's his business, not mine.

I work hard. I don't cheat.
If my wife cries
it's onion or ammonia.
We live well.
The baby changed nothing.

We swat till my wife
collapses. I shout
and growl. Still
the yellow jackets come,
late at night

they crawl from the baseboard.
At dawn they're beneath
my wife's feet
as she steps from the shower.
And on me, while I sleep.

From the Emerald City to the Mountain of Quaff (or This Must be Kansas)

Go out and get that long face lost, you say.
Bury me in Jerusalem, I reply.

I want to be one of the first to rise,
like yeast on a rock in the desert,

among iron stones, hills filled with brass,
in a land of olive oil and honey —

wrapped in silver and gold,
where water eats fire

and fire drowns water, and the angel
of the presence outlasts them both.

Or if poetry must be delirious and weird,
or even a prophetic frenzy,

then bury me in absurdia,
where the lemons bloom.

The Moment

She kneels like a shuffling penitent,
but no ecstasy to reach, only
a swaying agony. I gather
in my arms the brown-haired pygmy goat
to cradle her. In a lush landscape
she chose to nibble poisonous leaves,
perhaps the shiny rhododendron.

Just ten days before, I held our dog
as the vet eased her old way to death,
a surprising sudden heaviness
against my thigh. Why not a lightening
as life leaves? But this one, the pygmy
goat left in our care, suffers pinching
poison that shocks the compact body.

The pert knobbled head sways. I hold tight —
Don't die, little one, don't die! —
but cannot hold life in with frail arms.
A deep shuddering, last breath exhaled
into stillness, my empty embrace
gathering all those I have *not* held
into the moment of their dying.

Turning of the Year

We never know if the turn
is into the home stretch.
We call it that—a stretch
of place and time—
with vision of straining,
racing. We acknowledge
each turn with cheers
though we don't know
how many laps remain.
But we can hope the course
leads on far and clear
while the horses have strength
and balance on their lean legs,
fine-tuned muscles, desire
for the length of the run.
Some may find the year smooth,
others stumble at obstacles
along the way. We never know
if the finish line will be reached
after faltering, slowing,
or in mid-stride, leaping forward.

The Miner's Wife

The woman who went tight-lipped
and white when the siren blew

had long since postponed laughter
until her world could become clean.

She washed windows and smutty curtains,
daily scrubbed the steps. She washed

dishes at Rose's Café for the
lunch-hour rush, and washed school

uniforms every other night.
Like a labor of Hercules

was her scouring in the coal-mining
town, until she found in the laundry

a hole in her dead husband's sock
and wept into the siren's silence.

Villanelle: As You Seek Truth

As you seek truth in a chaos of lies
the city's clamor becomes desert where
you sift sand, winnow out all but the wise.

In the uniformity of franchise
wasteland, you are blinded by billboard glare
as you seek truth in a chaos of lies.

Since in sermons, statistics, slick advice,
one word of truth, one poem, might lie snared,
you sift sand, winnow out all but the wise.

Rainbow wigs, dreams sold for gain, a disguise
of time, of greed — disguise to be laid bare
as you seek truth in a chaos of lies.

From city masks you turn to dunes that rise
with shifting shapes, a wind-blown strand, and there
you sift sand, winnow out all but the wise.

This Herculean task you organize
into a harvest of gems, pure and rare.
As you seek truth in a chaos of lies
you sift sand, winnow out all but the wise.

Middle Earth

Down under farm fields
of this middle earth —
beneath pock-marked mud,
rows of burnt straw, and
one black Hereford
bull standing belly
deep in a small pond —
sit ordinary
young men, two of them,
two voluntary
hotages to a
midwest minefield of
missiles. These clean-cut
young men are programmed
to turn together
upon command
two keys in a red
metal box just as
the computer is
programmed to give them
that brief command for
Armageddon.
                But
now our helpless trust
must rest with just one
young man, George, who
expects one day to
have to turn that key.
He has to be careful,
calm, and conscientious.
His buddy, after
all, has just been court-
martialled for turning
a submachine gun
on a dog.

The Red Sofa

Tired of the hotel's restaurant fare
we slip through its revolving door
and lollygag around the French Quarter
in search of culinary promise.

We linger in front of
a furnishings storefront
admire the sleek design of a curvy red sofa:
After a couple of weeks of looking at that
in your living room
you'll want to take it outside and shoot it!
blurts the bag lady
pushing her cart past us.
Startled, we laugh and stroll off.

Today, leaning back on my red sofa
the middle-aged bag lady plops down
next to me and
warns about summer's curvy
French Quarter
al fresco feasts…

Dreams of Helgoland

In the play
Copenhagen
actors playing
Heisenberg and Bohr
discuss excursions to
Helgoland

and I wander toward
my childhood
and my father's stories of his youth
as a *Matrose* – a sailor.

After the start of the
second World War
there was no civilian German
fleet left. Merchant ships became rescue and spy ships
under the command of the German Navy.
However, my father insisted that
he was always a civilian sailor on a trade ship,
an Austrian whose rescue ship – *ein Lazarettschiff* – sank
during the Allied bombing of Hamburg.

He told stories about travels to places like
Trondheim and Helgoland where
Heisenberg conceived his
quantum mechanics breakthrough in 1925.

Heisenberg and Bohr discuss
nuclear fission in 1941's Copenhagen,
and a *Lazarettschiff* cruises the harbor.

Reading the Great Poets
to Cockroaches by Candlelight

Once, I stayed up all night reading Blake
to a cockroach by candlelight. He loved it.
He told his friends. Soon there were so
many in my room, I had to remain on good
terms with them. Later, I tried Coleridge—
the Ancient Mariner—a big hit! Cockroaches
have long attention spans. After Wordsworth,
they seemed wistful. It was Shelley, yes; Byron,
no. Keats made them weep. Poe drove them
mad!

8-1/2 X 11

   I'm staring at a sheet of white
paper—blank, typewriter paper—that's
lying on my desk, and I notice how much
it looks like a frozen, snow-covered
lake as seen from the air. I am a bush
pilot searching for someone lost in the
wastes of the far north—a hunter who
hasn't returned, who hasn't been heard
from for weeks—when suddenly out of
the miles of forest and frozen tundra, I
find this: a perfectly rectangular white
lake in the middle of nowhere. How can
this be? It is not on any of the maps,
no one has ever mentioned it, and I
have been flying over this country
for years.

Then Came the Rain

– for Rick, July 1960-August 2006

I read each word
twisted inside out
as that sinking feeling
rushes up my body

I can hear your voice quivering
behind your secret
Goodbye My Love, you've typed
in the subject box of my email

By the time you read this it'll be too late

They find you Friday morning
after I call the police,
and break down your door
while I, on hold, 3,000 miles away
hear the details of your death
So cold, so clinical
So lonely you must have been
waiting there for three days
for someone to come and claim you

I buy plants, soil, fertilizer, grass seed, and rocks
pack them in the trunk of my car
then till the soil of my front lawn
kneading its dried veins with my bare hands
I glaze each new leaf with rain water
dust the flowers
and sow my garden in an emerald mist

I can smell the magnolias
as I bend beneath an August sun
trying desperately to redecorate the world
making it beautiful enough for you
to come back.

Presbyterian Hospital ICU, 11:11 p.m.
from "The Air Is Full Of Our Cries"

Dad, can you hear me. Daddy, are you there?

Yes, but they can't know it. My son, now 24. The girl, now 22, conceived by another man, a Slav, my wife's lover when we were traveling in my reunion with the Balkans and stayed for six weeks in Skopje. I didn't learn that until she told me, in the course of one of our major conflicts. "She's not even yours, you weakling! And I have never had such good sex as I had with Vlad, not before and certainly not since!" Fair enough, I thought then and now. I'd had my share of strange. Besides, I loved my daughter, had raised her, educated her, and she acknowledged me as her father even after Janie told her about the Slav. "You're my father, no matter what," she said, weeping. About my son, there'd been no doubt. Conceived in a spasm on a ship bound for England, our lovemaking to and fro with the ocean's swells. Yes, that during one of our happy periods. Sunny he was at birth, sunny ever since, with only the occasional adolescent rebellion and fender-bender to mar his passage. Now he worked as a fledgling broker. The daughter, tempestuous but kind and sensitive, holds an entry-level job at the CBS affiliate in Chicago, where I'd grown up. The South Side of lore: blacks, micks, Jews, dagos, all of us sorts in one big stew of resentments and ambitions. That taught me early on to fight only those battles you might win, to cut deals, to persist. The kids had been present through all their parents' snaky progress toward what we hoped would be if not golden, at least comfortable, old age. But then came the road's s-curve, the truck. I wish I could see the children, gauge their solicitude, whether feigned or true, and now I sense their mother coming in.

Oh, glad you came now, Mrs. Bleecker Do you have a minute....

Shuffling noises, an air-puff from a pulled curtain? Fragments drift to me, like autumn leaves on a still pond, or scent from a distant woman.

"...must...hard...how can we...decision...I must . . . I won't. . . Me, either...

The air puff again. Is someone near? Touching me? Is it a caress? A tear on my cheek? More puffs. Janie's voice saying they have to go now for a while. It's always dark, but I infer it must be evening. Another phantom kiss... Nothing then but the whirring of machines. Is my sensing ability fading? Something seems to touch me. Vitals check? A pat? A hand clasp? Darkness palpable... I could be again. I wish I could taste single-malt Scotch and red wine and roast beef and crème brûlée and oysters and melons and ice cream and good tomatoes and crispy fries, and hear the sound of waves against a sailboat's hull and the wing beat of flushed quail rising, a symphony playing the Leningrad score and Tosca and Miles, Thelonius Monk, the Duke, Tom Rush, B.B., Willie, Reba, Placido, Julian Bream, the Goldberg Variations, Lady Day, Ella, Motown, Springsteen, U2, ColdPlay Beatles and Stones, Rodgers and Hart and Hammerstein, names and more names, Baldwin, Ellison, Morrison, Angelou, Stones, JFK, RFK, MLK, and movies, Casablanca and Chinatown, Almadovar's breakdowns, and Streep and Nicholson, Scorsese, DeNiro, Ephron, Spielberg, all present in here somewhere, along with the books, the Russians, Woolf and the Bloomsbury bunch, Hem and Scott and Whiskey Bill Faulkner, Oates, the two McCarthys, Bellow, Roth, the Romantics, *The New Yorker*, Seinfeld cracking wise, Masterpiece Theater's cool solemnity, so much more, Still's color fields, the descending blocks of Rothko, Picasso's crook-ed visions, O'Keefe, Giacometti, Caravaggio, Warhol's madness and Pollack's drips, and the odors scented now, of orange blossoms, of fresh asphalt, of burning leaves, of new-mown grass, of gunpowder, of incense and sweat, and of sweet sweat accompanying orgasm, of a long kiss, so much, in a twirly cosmos from somewhere in me, all of it, the short trek I/we take, destination uncertain, until the path either peters out in an unfathomable gloom or on another side, of clouded sunlight, of a new taking-on, like the slow giving of yourself to someone you truly care about. Oh, my, yes. If only . . . □

Moving the Clock Backwards

October 28, 2007
– *for TZW*

O Mouse, do you know
the way out of this pool?
Lewis Carroll, *Alice in Wonderland*

I wind
the clock hands
counter clockwise,
backwards in time,
before my husband's nouns and verbs
disappeared down the White Rabbit's hole.
My husband and I perch at the edge
where the rabbit raced,
where words tumbled,
The rabbit-hole went
straight on like a tunnel…

Damn infernal rabbit
Down, down, down
Do cats eat bats?
Do bats eat cats?

Again, I wind
the clock hands backwards,
not too far,
which way which way,
the little and big hands race.

If went by words
we can come back by them,
it flashed across my mind.
which way which way
where sun slants into his study.

Answering the Knock

The poet answers the knock,
throws open the door to welcome the muse.
It's the landlord screaming for rent;
a wife from years ago, cursing;
the man in a dingy suit
who collects unpaid bills for half
the merchants on the street.

Again and again the poet
jumps up from his chair,
drags wet from his bath,
leaps from between a lover's legs,
or rushes with tomato soup
smeared across his chin
to answer the knock,
till he sees *Death* slouched on the sill,
humming a familiar tune.

Each Small Bone

One at a time he fashions
each small bone,
each tight sinew,
each ligament.
He spends days
carving her jaw,
sanding down her brow.
Her throat he tunes
with wire thin as truth;
turns each breast
on a tender lathe.
The feet take forever.

Roster

This death is bought with mangos,
that one with roasted pigs.
Some are quiet, some loud.
This one repeats itself
like pain. This death,
ecstasy; that one, defeat.
One by fire, one by sword;
two from love,
three from neglect.
A babe followed by
a twisted, old man.
A woman in her prime;
a muddied, bloodied PFC.
Cain follows Abel,
followed by all the *begets*,
the Son of God,
the lamb.
Mozart, Rasputin, Dachau;
the neighbor to the left.
Next.

Yahrzeit: Death's Anniversary Dream

Last night, my father
stood naked like me:

His penis, smaller than I'd imagined,
his chest indented like a battered suitcase.
An asterisk of saber scars
engraved on his stomach pogroms he'd survived.
No tailor had altered
his fretted skin to fit.

To his left, two paces back,
her clothes heaped like plucked feathers
of a *Shabbas* chicken,
my mother stood on feet
poured without a mold,
bound up in veins.
Her breasts, puffed out gray poached eggs.
Her pubic hair twined like brambles
beneath belly folds for each child.

All their years recorded.

When I saw them,
I covered my groin with both hands.
They covered their mouths.

Pussan, 1951

From a hilltop
north of the harbor,
I watched beside a Swedish nurse
the ascending moon blanch and contract.
We pulled dried octopus skin between clenched teeth,
drank sake from clay jars,
let our bodies thresh the stubbled incline.

On the way back in a borrowed jeep,
sniper fire riddled the radiator,
spare tire, the nurse's blue knapsack-purse.
Five miles down the road,
to get us back behind friendly lines,
I pissed in the radiator,
dry as a picked-over bone.

ACKNOWLEDGMENTS

Catherine Anderson: "Train from the South" from *Southern Indiana Review*, 2010. "Womanhood" and "Midwifery" from *The Work of Hands* by Catherine Anderson, Perugia Press, 2000.

Thomas Fox Averill: "To Appreciate a Garden" from *scissors and spackle, a journal of the written word,* Vol. I, Number VII, 2012.

Stanley E. Banks: "An Offbeat Singer" from *Willow Review,* 2012.

Hadara Bar-Nadav: "Write Paris out of the Pictures" from *Kenyon Review,* 2009. "Black and White" and "Egg and Envy" from A *Glass of Milk to Kiss Goodnight* by Hadara Bar-Nadav, *Margie*/Intuit House, 2007.

Kelly Barth: "Witnessing" from *My Almost Certainly Real Imaginary Jesus* by Kelly Barth, Arktoi Books, an imprint of Red Hen Press, 2012.

Bill Bauer: "Pear Season" from *Pear Season and the Boy Who Ate Dandelions* by Bill Bauer, Mid-America Press, Inc., 2006. "The Farmer's Widow at His Grave" from *Promises in the Dust* by Bill Bauer, BkMk Press, 1995.

Phyllis Becker: "How I Came to Love Jazz" from *How I Came to Love Jazz* by Phyllis Becker, Helicon Nine Editions, 2008.

Carl Bettis: "The Future Is Now" from *Thorny Locust,* Vol.18:1. "Dust" from *The Same,* Vol.9:2.

Boisseau, Michelle. "In Her Parachute-Silk Wedding Gown" from *No Private Life* by Michelle Boisseau, Vanderbilt University Press, 1990. "Done" from *Trembling Air,* Copyright 2003 by Michelle Boisseau. Reproduced with the permission of the University of Arkansas Press, www.uapress.com. "Death Gets Into the Suburbs" from *Poetry,* January 2012.

Catherine Browder: "Conquistadors" from *Number One,* University of Missouri-Kansas City, Spring, 1997.

Carol Gorski Buckels: "Before the Eclipse" from *Well Versed – Literary Works 2012,* Columbia Chapter Missouri Writers' Guild.

G. S. Sharat Chandra: "Facts of Life," "Mount Pleasant, USA," "Stillness," "Poets in Groups" from *Family of Mirrors* by G. S. Sharat Chandra, BkMk Press, 1993.

Maril Crabtree: "Breaking the Drought" from *Moving On* by Maril Crabtree, Pudding House Press, 2010.

Brian Daldorph: "The Been-To" from *Senegal Blue* by Brian Daldorph, 219 Press, 2003.

Joseph DeLuca: "Bathsheba…" from *I-70 Review*.

Jan Duncan-O'Neal: "Requiem for a Prodigal Daughter" from *Mid-America Poetry Review*, 2006.

Sharon Eiker: "Dance by the Light of the Moon" from *Poets At Large*, Helicon Nine Editions.

B. H. Fairchild: "The Gray Man" from *Usher: Poems* by B. H. Fairchild. Copyright © 2009 by B. H. Fairchild. Used by permission of W.W. Norton & Company, Inc. "Old Men Playing Basketball," "Kansas," "The Himalayas," and "Airlifting Horses" from *The Art of the Lathe*. Copyright © 1998 by B. H. Fairchild. Reprinted with the permission of The Permissions Company, Inc., on behalf of Alice James Books, www.alicejamesbooks.org

Greg Field: "A Brief Discussion of Heisenberg's Uncertainty Principle," "How a Bird Is Born," and "The Sea is the Longest Breath" from *New Letters*, 1998, 2007, 1988. "Solutions" from *Thorny Locust*.

Dennis Finnell: "Silent Running" from *New Letters*, 2009.

Diane Glancy: "Father, My Father" from *It Was Then* by Diane Glancy, Mammoth Publishers, 2012.

C. W. Gusewelle: Excerpt from *The Rufus Chronicle* by C. W. Gusewelle, Kansas City Star Books, 1996.

Tina Hacker: "Sheba" from *Kansas City Voices*, 2007; "Where the Chips Fall" and "Sheba" from *Cutting It* by Tina Hacker, The Lives You Touch Publications, 2010.

Jamie Lynn Heller: "The Previous Owner" from *Prairie Schooner*, Fall 2011.

Ernest Hemingway: "Champs d'Honneur," "Mitrailliatrice" and "Riparto d'Assalto" from *Poetry*, January 1923. These and "Montparnasse," "Night comes with soft and drowsy plumes" and "Schwarzwald" from *88 Poems* by Ernest Hemingway, Harcourt Brace Jovanovich, 1979.

Bill Hickok: "Mahler and Me" from *The Kansas City Star*. "To Be," "Tattoo," "Dragon's Breath" and "Mahler and Me" from *The Woman Who Shot Me* by Bill Hickok, Whirlybird Press, 2011.

Frank Higgins: "On the Beach at Night" from *The Kansas City Star*. "Starting from Ellis Island" from *Dacotah Territory* and from *Starting from Ellis Island* by Frank Higgins, BkMk Press, 1979.

H. L. Hix: "Summer" and "Fall" from *Shadows of Houses* by H. L. Hix, Etruscan Press, 2005.

Dan Jaffe: "The Forecast" from *Prairie Schooner.* "The Cannonball" from *Dan Freeman* by Dan Jaffe, U. Of Nebraska Press, 1967. "Looking for the Foreman" and "Dirty Song" from *On the Way to the Polls* by Dan Jaffe, City Light Publishing, 2009. "Menorah Hospital" from *Round for One Voice* by Dan Jaffe, University of Arkansas Press, 1988.

Judith Bader Jones: "The Knob" from *Explorations.* "An Empty Barn" from *Moon Flowers on the Fence* by Judith Bader Jones, Finishing Line Press, 2010.

Robert C. Jones: "Wood Carver" from *Dreams to Sell* by Robert C. Jones, Mid-America Press, 2009. "Encantation" from *Within this Center: A Sketchbook of Poems* by Robert C. Jones, Mid-America Press, 1975.

Silvia Kofler: "The Red Sofa" from *The Kansas City Star* and from *Radioactive Musings* by Silvia Kofler, UD Press, 2008.

Patricia Lawson: "Greasy Joan" from *The Same.*

Deborah Linton: "Mannington, West Virginia, November 23, 1968 – (AP)" from *Kansas City Outloud*, BkMk Press, 1975.

Barbara Loots: "The Boat Builder" from *Measure*, 2008. "Handling the Evidence" from *New Letters*, 1985.

Crystal MacLean-Field: "Thirteen Pictures of a Sister," "Woman Found in an Art Gallery," "Prufrock Was Wrong," "Dear Mother, I Will Never Be Enough" from *My Sister's Leather Bag* by Crystal MacLean-Field, Mid-America Press, 1982.

Lindsey Martin-Bowen: "From the Emerald City to the Mountain of Quaff" from *Kansas City Voices*, 2007.

Hilary Masters: Excerpt from *Last Stands: Notes from Memory* by Hilary Masters, David Godine, Boston, 1982.

Jo McDougall: "What We Need," "Threads," "Telling Time" from *Dirt* by Jo McDougall, Autumn House Press, 2001. "Taxidermy" from *Satisfied With Havoc* by Jo McDougall, Autumn House Press, 2004. All poems reprinted with permission from the author and Autumn House Press.

Patricia Cleary Miller: "Eleanor Elkins Widener Builds Her Library" from *Potpourri* and *"The Maori Never Age" and Other Selected Harvard Poems* by Patricia Cleary Miller, Covington, 2012.

Philip Miller: "Like a Tree" from *Rattapallax*; "Missing" and "The Other" from *Thorny Locust*; these three poems later from *Branches Snapping* by Philip Miller, Helicon Nine Editions, 2003. "How It All Begins" from *Hard Freeze* by Philip Miller, BkMk Press, 1994. "Other People's Fathers" from *Father's Day*, winner of 1995 The Ledge Press chapbook contest.

Wayne Miller: "In the Barracks: A Found Poem," "CPR," "[The child's cry is a light that comes on in the house]" from *The City, Our City* by Wayne Miller, Minneapolis, Milkweed Editions, 2011. Copyright 2011 by Wayne Miller. Reprinted with permission from Milkweed Editions. www.milkweed.org

Al Ortolani: "Performing the High Wire" from *Ramshackle Review.*

David Owen: Excerpt from "The Dime Store Floor" from *The New Yorker*, January 25, 2010. Reprinted with permission from the author.

H. C. Palmer: "In the Tall Grass of a Landing Zone" from *The Flint Hills Review.* "Counting Boys in a Truck" from *The New Mexico Poetry Review.* "In Caravaggio's Saint John the Baptist in the Wilderness" from *Ekphrasis.*

Anika Paris: "Then Came the Rain" from *Woven Voices: Three Generations of Puertoriqueña Poets Look at Their American Lives*, Scapegoat Press, 2012.

Steve Paul: "Shore Birds" from *New Letters*, 2008, winner of the Stanley Hanks Memorial Prize from the St. Louis Poetry Center.

Susan Peters: "Chiaroscuro" from *Kansas City Voices.*

Michael Pritchett: Excerpt from "Trinity" from *The Venus Tree* by Michael Pritchett, University of Iowa Press, 1988.

Alan R. Proctor: "Old Highway 9" from *Loon 6.*

David Ray: "Thanks, Robert Frost" from *Poet's Choice*, 1980, and *The Touched Life* by David Ray, Scarecrow Press, 1982. "Legacy" from *Wool Highways* by David Ray, Helicon Nine Editions, 1993. "After Tagore" from *Thorny Locust*, 1995. "To a Child of Baghdad" from *Kangaroo Paws* by David Ray, Thomas Jefferson U. Press, 1994. "Return to the Desert" from *When* by David Ray, Howling Dog Press, 2007.

Judy Ray: "Turning of the Year" from *Thorny Locust*, 2010. "Villanelle As You Seek Truth" from *Pebble Rings* by Judy Ray, Greenfield Review Press, 1980. "The Miner's Wife" and "Middle Earth" from *Pigeons in the Chandeliers* by Judy Ray, Timberline Press, 1993.

Samuel Cyrus Ray: "Looking Ahead," "Is There Time to Compose?" and "Late Words" from *New Letters.*

Trish Reeves: "The Bedroom Too Near the Church Bell in the Duomo" and "Picture at Impact" from *New Letters.* "The Silver Coin" from *Ploughshares.*

Carl Rhoden: "Reading the Great Poets to Cockroaches by Candlelight" from *Any Key Review.* "8½ x 11" from *Coal City Review.*

Richard Rhodes: Excerpt from *The Inland Ground* by Richard Rhodes, Atheneum, New York, 1970.

Shirley Rickett: "Her Dress" from *Nimrod*. "Eternal People" from *Antietam Review*.

Andrés Rodríguez: "Papa Cayo" from *Night Song* by Andrés Rodríguez, Tia Chucha Press, 1994. "Nacimiento" from *The Kansas City Star*, December 20, 2009.

Elizabeth Rowe: "Solo Flight" (in earlier version) from *Flying Magazine,* 1999.

Vernon Rowe: "MRI of a Poet's Brain" from *Sea Creatures* by Vernon Rowe, Whirlybird Press, 1995. "After Frost's Grindstone," "The Horseman" and "The Country Doctor" from *The Ride* by Vernon Rowe, Whirlybird Press, 2011.

Ann Slegman: "It's Cool to be in India" from *Conversation* by Ann Slegman, Helicon Nine Editions, 2004.

Mbembe Milton Smith: "Ancestry as Reality," "American History, Popular Version," "Nostalgia of the Mud," "Allegory of the Bebop Walk," "Something Else They Say," from *Mbembe: Selected Poems*, BkMk Press, 1986.

Robert Stewart: "Roughing In" and "Waiting for the Plumber" from *Plumbers* by Robert Stewart, BkMk Press, 1988. "No Theory" from *Notre Dame Review*, 2002. "What a Poem Can Teach Us," excerpt from *On Swerving: The Way of William Stafford*, Literary House Press, 2007. "The Narrow Gate" from *New Letters*, 2009.

Polly W. Swafford: "Denial" from *Rockhurst Review*, 2006. "On Sunday" from *Mid-America Poetry Review*, 2007-08.

James Tate: "Graveside," "The Lost Pilot," "Up Here," "Coda" and "The Blue Booby" from *Selected Poems* © 1991 by James Tate. Reprinted by permission of Wesleyan University Press.

Alarie Tennille: "*Éléphants Nageurs*" from *Margie*, 2008. "*Éléphants Nageurs*" and "Natural Order" both from *Spiraling into Control* by Alarie Tennille, The Lives You Touch Publications, 2010.

Whitney Terrell: Excerpt from *The King of Kings County* by Whitney Terrell, Viking/Penguin, 2005.

Roderick Townley: "Rue des Halles" from *Poets at Large*, Helicon Nine Editions, 1997.

Wyatt Townley: "Keeping Your Place" and "The Fountain" from *The Afterlives of Trees* by Wyatt Townley, Woodley Press, 2011. "Reversing a Decision" from *Poets at Large*, Helicon Nine Editions, 1997.

William Trowbridge: "Stark Weather" from *Enter Dark Stranger* by William Trowbridge, University of Arkansas Press, 1989. "My Father's Laugh" and "Fool Noir" from *Ship of Fool* by William Trowbridge, Red Hen Press, 2011. "Kong Bares His Soul Regarding Miss Tyrannasaura Regina" from *The Complete Book of Kong* by William Trowbridge, Southeast Missouri State University Press, 2003.

Donna Trussell: "Remember Me as a Writer, Not a Survivor" from *Newsweek*, February, 2006. "Dreams Indexed" from *New Letters*. "Yellow Jackets" from *What's Right About What's Wrong* by Donna Trussell, Helicon Nine Editions, 2008.

Leslie Ullman: "Mind Trades Shadows with the Clouds" and "By Night, Penelope" from *Progress on the Subject of Immensity* by Leslie Ullman, forthcoming from University of New Mexico Press, 2013. "1945" and "Prayer" from *Slow Work through Sand* by Leslie Ullman, University of Iowa Press, 1998.

Gloria Vando: "My 90-Year-Old Father and My Husband Discuss Their Trip to the Moon" and "Flag Day at Union Cemetery" from *New Letters*. "The Fall," "new shoes and an old flame" and "Flag Day at Union Cemetery" from *Shadows & Supposes* by Gloria Vando, Arte Público Press, 2002.

Maryfrances Wagner: "The Last Shot" from *The Birmingham Review*. "In the Same Place" from *Jam Today*. "Wounded in Chu Lai" from *Red Silk* by Maryfrances Wagner, MidAmerica Press, 1999. "All the Time Running" from *Mid-American Poetry Review*.

Sylvia Wheeler: "My Daughter, Her Boyfriend, My Poem" from *City Limits* by Sylvia Wheeler, BkMk Press, 1973. "August Letter" from *Dancing Alone* by Sylvia Wheeler, BkMk Press,1991.

Thomas Zvi Wilson: "Answering the Knock," "Each Small Bone," "Roster," "*Yahrzeit*: Death's Anniversary Dream" and "Pussan, 1951" from *Deliberate and Accidental Acts*, BkMk Press, 1996.

Carrie Allison is a writer who has lived in the Kansas City area since birth. Her poems and articles have appeared in a variety of magazines and journals. Her poetry chapbook *Pointing Toward Home* was published by Mid-America Press.

Catherine Anderson is the author of *The Work of Hands* (Perugia Press) and *In the Mother Tongue* (Alice James Books). Her poems have appeared in the *Southern Review, Prairie Schooner, Many Mountains Moving, The Midwest Quarterly,* and in many anthologies. She works with Kansas City's growing and vibrant refugee and immigrant communities.

Thomas Fox Averill, an O. Henry Award winning short story writer, is Writer-in-residence at Washburn University of Topeka. His third novel, *rode* (University of New Mexico Press), was named Outstanding Western Novel of 2011 as part of the Western Heritage Awards. His most recent work, "Garden Plots," is a series of short-short stories, prose poems, and poetry on the subject of gardens and the human relationship with nature.
"I taught for the University of Kansas at the Edwards campus, and am such a frequent visitor to Kansas City that I claim citizenship."

Janet Banks's poems have appeared in *The Kansas City Star* and other respected literary publications. Her first book of poetry was titled *Stewed Soul,* and her second book, *On the Edge of Urban,* is scheduled to be published soon.
"If someone were to print out a map of Kansas City, Missouri, and do an archaeological dig, they would find culture unseen by the naked eye."

Stanley E. Banks is Assistant Professor and Artist-in-Residence at Avila College in Kansas City, Missouri. He has won several awards, including a Langston Hughes Prize for Poetry (1981) and a National Endowment for the Arts Fellowship/Grant for Poetry (1989). He has four published books, and an upcoming book is titled *Blue Issues.*
"When I think about Kansas City, Missouri, I am truly grateful for the inspirational and spirited legacy of my grandfather who was a World War I Veteran and my grandmother who was a Vine Street bootlegger from the 1930s to 1960s."

Walter Bargen has published fourteen books of poetry, the most recent being *Days Like This Are Necessary: New & Selected Poems* (2009)

248

and *Endearing Ruins/Liebenswerte Ruinen* (2012). He was appointed the first poet laureate of Missouri (2008-2009).
www.walterbargen.com
"Along the avenues in the City of Fountains, horses reared and dolphins breached spouting the moist glitter of the eternal, where I would stroll an equally endless time."

Hadara Bar-Nadav is the author of *A Glass of Milk to Kiss Goodnight* (*Margie*/Intuit House, 2007), awarded the Margie Book Prize; *The Frame Called Ruin* (forthcoming, New Issues 2012), Runner Up for the Green Rose Prize; and *Lullaby (with Exit Sign)*, awarded the Saturnalia Book Prize (forthcoming, Saturnalia Books 2013). She is Associate Professor of English at the University of Missouri-Kansas City, where she directs the Creative Writing Program.
"My family has found great friends, great art, great music, and great food in Kansas City, a city of many gifts that continues to welcome us."

Kelly Barth lives with her partner Lisa Grossman in Lawrence, Kansas. She grew up in Raytown, Missouri, and graduated from UMKC with a degree in creative writing/journalism. She was a fiction fellow in the University of Montana's creative writing program and has received fellowships from the Missouri Arts Council and the Kansas Arts Commission. *My Almost Certainly Real Imaginary Jesus* (Arktoi Books/Red Hen, 2012) is her first book.
"My favorite haunt in Kansas City is the Rozelle Court at the Nelson-Atkin's Museum of Art, where my mother first took me when it was still a roofless courtyard."

Bill Bauer grew up in the Westport area of Kansas City. A Vietnam veteran, he co-founded an international insurance firm that defends the First Amendment rights of the media, and is the author of four books of poetry and short fiction. His current work is posted at billbauerpoetry.com.
"Few moments are as rich as a crisp Kansas City autumn after a wet summer or falling asleep to the sounds and scents of a spring thunderstorm under the city's great trees."

Conger Beasley, Jr. has published in many forms, including essays, poetry, short fiction, travel accounts, and the novel. His most recent work is a book-length, mock-epic narrative poem entitled *Holy Warriors* (Dodo Bird Publishing, 2010). He currently is ghost writing the autobiography of a Chiricahua Apache elder named Watson

"Bill" Mythlo, the last Apache born in captivity in Fort Marion, Florida, in 1886.

Phyllis Becker is coordinator of the Riverfront Readings series in Kansas City featuring local and regional writers. Her book *How I Came to Love Jazz* was published in 2008 (Helicon Nine Editions). Her poems have also been set to jazz on the CD, *Poetry of Love*, produced by Jazz artist Angela Hagenbach.
"Kansas City is a great city and one the best kept secrets in the United States... I kind of like it that way."

Carl Bettis is a web developer, poet and member of the Riverfront Readings Committee. His work has appeared in *The Same, Thorny Locust* and other periodicals, as well as the anthology *Chance of a Ghost* (Helicon Nine Editions, 2005). He can be found online at www.carlbettis.com
"Whether you go for literary, visual or performance art, you'll find what you're looking for in Kansas City, a town juicy with creativity."

Michelle Boisseau received NEA poetry fellowships in 1989 and 2010. Her most recent books of poems, published by University of Arkansas Press, are *A Sunday in God-Years* (2009) and *Trembling Air* (2003, a PEN USA finalist). Her other collections are *Understory* (Morse Prize, Northeastern University Press) and *No Private Life* (Vanderbilt University Press). Her textbook, *Writing Poems* (Longman), is in its 8th edition. She is a professor in the MFA program at the University of Missouri-Kansas City.

Catherine Browder is a fiction writer and playwright, with two published collections and a *feuillet*. Her stories have appeared in, or won awards from *Glimmer Train, Nimrod, Shenandoah, New Letters, Green Mountains Review, Prairie Schooner* and elsewhere. She has received fellowships from the NEA and the Missouri Arts Council, and is an advisory editor for *New Letters* magazine where her book reviews appear.
"My Kansas City is a Mecca for immigrants (many of whom I've taught) as well as urban pioneers; a home to vibrant young artists who have revitalized the West Bottoms and Crossroads with storefront theaters, pocket art galleries and trendy restaurants; and contrary to the notions of 'Coastals' who have never visited, it is anything but flat: a vast, spread out metropolis, it pitches and rolls with limestone cliffs and hardwood trees, thriving at the convergence of two muscular rivers, the Missouri and the Kaw."

Carol Gorski Buckels writes poetry on a 20-acre hobby farm in Rocheport, Missouri, which she and her husband Steve share with 3 dogs and 3 cats. She graduated from UMKC (B.A. English) and worked at *The Kansas City Star* when she lived in Kansas City in the 1970s and 80s.
"Compared to my east coast birthplace – Rome, New York – Kansas City was the 'Big City', with its bronze and marble statues and fountains, museums, highways and skyscrapers; but also 'the West' – the grassy pastureland where I first owned a horse – a honey colored mare, trained to rear up by a cowboy – the city where I first snuck into a bar to hear poetry read to the accompaniment of beer and the blues."

G. S. Sharat Chandra (1935 – 2000), born and raised in India, held law degrees from both India and Canada. He immigrated to the United States in the 1960s, became a writer of fiction and poetry, and published seven books, including *Family of Mirrors* (BkMk Press) and the short story collection, *Sari of the Gods* (Coffee House). He taught creative writing at the University of Missouri-Kansas City.

Maril Crabtree has made Kansas City her home since 1964. Her poetry has appeared in numerous anthologies and journals including *Kalliope, The DMQ Review, Steam Ticket, Coal City Review,* and *Third Wednesday,* and in two chapbooks. She is Poetry Co-Editor for *Kansas City Voices,* a visual and literary arts magazine.
"Through the decades, I have seen Kansas City dance, plod, sparkle, trudge, almost drown, almost shrivel, wander aimlessly and march purpose-fully – but always, always persevere with a welcoming heart."

Caryn Curtis writes: My 1976 arrival in Kansas City was preceded by my marriage, in the Marshall Islands, to a Missourian. Raised in the "Rocket City" of Huntsville, Alabama, I grew up amidst Scientists, Engineers and Cotton farmers. I learned that we attain dreams when we reach in community, walking on the moon. My motivation is to write expressing hope and joy.
"Kansas City has been a diverse blessing of people and seasonal natural beauty."

Brian Daldorph teaches at the University of Kansas and Douglas County Jail. He edits *Coal City Review.*
"The joys of Kansas City: half marathons in the morning, poetry at night!"

Joseph DeLuca is a poet who has lived and written in various cities throughout the world. Currently he resides in Kansas City, his hometown, with his wife and three children.

A Pushcart Nominee, **Jan Duncan-O'Neal** has had numerous poems published, including her chapbook, *Voices: Lost and Found* (The Lives You Touch Publications, 2011). A storyteller and retired librarian, she is currently an editor for *I-70 Review*. Born in Kansas City, Missouri, Jan now lives in Overland Park, Kansas with husband Bill. *"Kansas City's skyline takes my breath away, celebrates the arts, and inspires a grand community of writers – my kind of town!"*

John Mark Eberhart was born in 1960 in St. Joseph, Mo., a long stone's throw from the house in which Jesse James was assassinated. He is the author of two verse collections, *Night Watch* (2005) and *Broken Time* (2008).
"One of the things I love about Kansas City is it still feels open; it's in the middle of everything, so if escape is called for – you have one hell of a lot of options."

Sharon Eiker was born in rural Missouri on April 5, 1943. She is a visual artist, musician, and poet. Her definition of poetry is: The song of the soul sung to the beat of the heart. She believes a poem is not complete until at least one other person hears it. She has hosted The Writers Place open mike in Kansas City for twenty years.
"Kansas City is a small town. A person with tenacity will be able to meet every one of any consequence in the Arts in a very short time. Knowing and being known both are possible."

B. H. Fairchild is the author of *Early Occult Memory Systems of the Lower Midwest*, winner of the National Book Critics Circle Award and the Bobbitt Prize from the Library of Congress; *The Arrival of the Future; Local Knowledge;* and *The Art of the Lathe*, a finalist for the National Book Award and winner of the Kingsley Tufts Award and the William Carlos Williams Award. He now lives in California but remembers well his years in the Kansas City area and still returns to give readings.

José Faus's work appears in the anthologies *Primera Pagina: Poetry from the Latino Heartland* and *Cuentos del Centro: Stories from the Latino Heartland*, and forthcoming *In the black/In the red, Raritan, Luces y*

Sombras. He is the 2011 winner of Poets & Writers Maureen Egen Writers Exchange Award.

"Kansas City has been home for over 45 years to the point where its streets, peoples, smells and sites constitute the feeders of my creative DNA."

Charles Ferruzza was born and raised in Indianapolis. He graduated from both Butler University and the National Bartending School. He was written for many newspapers and magazines and his work has been published in several anthologies. He can frequently be heard on radio on KCUR-FM and KKFI-FM. He no longer drinks, smokes or collects things.

Greg Field is a writer, artist, and musician who lives in Independence, Missouri. His poetry has been published in numerous journals and anthologies. He is a percussionist with the band River Cow Orchestra. He co-edits the *I-70 Review*. His artwork is in private collections throughout the U.S.

"I was born in Kansas City and then began a journey that took me to Anchorage, Alaska, Las Vegas, Nevada, back to Anchorage and then back to Las Vegas again. But, I made my way back home to Kansas City where I can still experience the cycles of all four seasons like a master clock's heart beat."

Dennis Finnell has published *Red Cottage* which won the Juniper Prize, and *Belovèd Beast* and *The Gauguin Answer Sheet*, both from University of Georgia Press. His new book, *Pie 8*, won 2012 Bellday Poetry Prize. He has received grants and fellowships from the Vogelstein, Ragdale, and MacDowell Foundations.

"Kansas City is confluence, East meeting West, North, and South, kinetic centers where friends helped me cross streets, and still now do."

Diane Glancy, professor emeritus at Macalester College in St. Paul, Minnesota, is currently professor at Azusa Pacific University near Los Angeles. Her awards include two NEA fellowships, a Minnesota Book Award, an Oklahoma Book Award, and an American Book Award from the Before Columbus Foundation. Recent poetry collections are *Stories of the Driven World* (2010) and *It Was Then* (2011) from Mammoth Publishers, and a nonfiction work is *The Dream of a Broken Field* (2011, University of Nebraska Press).

"I was born in Kansas in 1941. My father came to Kansas City in 1928, and worked for the stockyards all his life...In the 1960s, the Armour plant in Kansas City was razed, and I went with him to see the empty lot where

Armour's had been...All these years later, I'm still writing about the stockyards. The wool skirt and sweater [in the poem] were purchased when I was a student at the University of Missouri."

C. W. Gusewelle has written 57 years for *The Kansas City Star*, as reporter, foreign editor, and columnist. His stories and essays have appeared in *Harper's, American Heritage* and many other magazines, journals and anthologies. He is the author of 12 books, and was awarded *The Paris Review's* 1977 Aga Khan Prize for Fiction. He has traveled widely in Europe, the Middle East and Siberia, but his heart's home has always been Kansas City.

Tina Hacker has a recently published chapbook titled *Cutting It* (The Lives You Touch Publications). A three-time Pushcart Prize nominee and Editor's Choice for two journals, she was a finalist in *New Letters* and George F. Wedge competitions. Her poetry has appeared in numerous journals and anthologies.
"Kansas City has a lively literary community, especially The Writers Place, which has provided me with abundant exposure to other poets and excellent opportunities for growth."

Lora Hawkins: Granddaughter to two local poets, Bill and Gloria Hickok, Lora studied English and theatre at Warren Wilson College. She earned her Masters degree at Brown University, and is currently teaching English in Kuwait.
Lora misses Kansas City's pork ribs and forsythia bushes.

Jamie Lynn Heller writes: I have two young girls, the perfect spouse, a high school counseling career I love, and I get to write. It's a productive day when I can squeeze in a half hour or so to devote to poetry.
"I have lived in or around this area my entire life and I love Kansas City, but I wonder sometimes how well it knows itself."

Ernest Hemingway (1899 – 1961), born in Oak Park, Illinois, was a cub reporter for *The Kansas City Star* for several months in 1917-18 when he learned good ground rules of writing from the *Star's* style sheet. He worked on two of his books, *A Farewell to Arms* and *Death in the Afternoon*, on later visits to the city. Hemingway's novels and short stories are considered American classics, and in 1954 he was awarded the Nobel Prize in Literature.

Bill Hickok's humorous articles and poems have appeared on the Op-Ed pages of *Cleveland Plain Dealer, The Kansas City Star, Newsday, Philadelphia Enquirer,* and in *Uncle* (the magazine for those who have given up), *The Same,* and on-line. *The Woman Who Shot Me* (Whirly-bird Press, 2011) is his first poetry collection. He is co-founder of The Writers Place, a literary center in Kansas City.
"After Julia Irene Kauffman's home run for the arts, K.C. rocks!"

Frank Higgins's play "The Sweet By 'n' By" was produced with Tony-winner Blythe Danner and Oscar-winner Gwyneth Paltrow, and "Black Pearl Sings!" was produced with Tony-winner Tonya Pinkins. His plays have been seen in New York, and across the country as well as in Vienna, Austria. His plays for young audiences include "Anansi the Spider and The Middle Passage" and "The Country of the Blind." His books of poetry include *Starting From Ellis Island* and *hello hello.* He teaches playwriting at the University of Missouri-Kansas City.

H. L. Hix's recent books include a "selected poems," *First Fire, Then Birds: Obsessionals 1985-2010* (Etruscan Press, 2010), and an essay collection, *Lines of Inquiry* (Etruscan Press, 2011). He lived in Kansas City from 1987-2002. His website is www.hlhix.com.
"If I have a spiritual home, it's Kansas City: I 'grew up' as a poet there by learning from my amazing colleagues in the visual arts at KCAI."

Dan Jaffe's last three books have been largely about music, jazz and classical. He has written more than 150 jazz poems, likely more than anyone else. In 2007 he was selected as an Elder Statesman of Kansas City Jazz. Jaffe has appeared with many of America's great jazz musicians. They include Mike Melvoin, Ira Sullivan, Bobby Watson, David Basse, Frank Smith, George Salisbury, Nicky Yarling, etc.
He calls Kansas City his home town, although he was born in New Jersey. Where else, he asks, could one find the same mix of music, letters, and great players?!

Judith Bader Jones's collection of short fiction, *Delta Pearls,* received The William Rockhill Nelson 2007 Fiction Award. Her chapbooks, *Moon Flowers on the Fence* (2010) and *The Language of Small Rooms* (2011), were published by Finishing Line Press of Georgetown, Kentucky.
"I have strong ties to the writing community of Kansas City, a place that supports poets when they write to make sense of their world."

Dr. Robert C. Jones was Professor of English at Central Missouri State University for 30 years, retiring in 1990. During this time he was awarded Fulbright Fellowships in Romania and Greece, and was first director of the Missouri London Program. He was editor and publisher of Mid-America Press for many years, and published the *Mid-America Poetry Review*. His poems have been published in periodicals throughout the country.

In addition to *Radioactive Musings* (2008), **Silvia Kofler**'s poems and translations have appeared in the *I-70 Review*, *OR*, *The Dirty Goat*, *The Book of Hopes and Dreams* (an anthology to benefit Spirit Aid), *The Sixth Surface: Steven Holl Lights the Nelson-Atkins Museum*, *travelin' music: A Poetic Tribute to Woody Guthrie*, and others.
"Kansas City offers everything larger cities have at an affordable, easy-going pace: a diverse artistic community, world-class museums and architecture, excellent restaurants, and incredible green spaces."

Patricia Lawson taught English at Kansas City Kansas Community College. She has published fiction and poetry in literary journals including *Pleiades*, *New Letters*, *BigCityLit*, *Rosebud*, *The Chariton Review*, *The Dalhousie Review*, *The Same*, and elsewhere. She co-authored, with the late Phil Miller, *Why We Love Our Cats and Dogs*. She is an associate editor of *The Same*.
"I would need a lot of adjectives to describe Kansas City but will go with five off the top of my head: friendly, scattered, accessible (socially, not geographically), and conservative with a liberal core."

Gary Lechliter's poetry has recently appeared in *Main Street Rag*, *New Mexico Poetry Review*, *Straylight*, *Tears in the Fence*, and *Wisconsin Review*. He has a recent book, *Foggy Bottoms: Poems about Myths and Legends*, published by Coal City Press.
"I met my wife in Kansas City. We enjoy the Nelson Art Gallery and The Plaza. We lived a mere mile from Truman Sports Complex, where I jogged and walked. I received my graduate degree from University of Missouri-Kansas City. I have enjoyed being a member of The Writers Place for many years. We still have great friends living in the city."

Deborah Linton writes: "I grew up in Kansas City and try to visit the city as often as possible. I wrote this poem for a class taught by Dan Jaffe. I remember in the poem as I first wrote it, I wrote "truthful as a wrinkle." Mr. Jaffe did not like that, so I changed it to its form that appears here."

The poems of **Barbara Loots** have appeared in a long list of agreeable publications, including *The Lyric, New Letters, Measure,* and *The Formalist,* and in anthologies such as *The Helicon Nine Reader, The Random House Treasury of Light Verse, The Random House Book of Poetry for Children,* and *The Muse Strikes Back.* She is included in a four-poet collection entitled *Landscapes with Women.*
"A forty-year career with Hallmark Cards – the veritable heart of my native city – provided the means for me to write poetry."

Crystal MacLean Field was born Crystal Joy Groulx in Michigan. Her two books of poems are *The Good Woman* (BkMk) and *My Sister's Leather Bag.* She taught workshops around the Kansas City area and taught at Penn Valley Community College. She died at age 49 in 1987. Her favorite place in Kansas City was the Nelson-Atkins Museum of Art.

Lindsey Martin-Bowen teaches at UMKC. Woodley Press/Washburn University published her *Standing on the Edge of the World,* named one of the *Top 10 Poetry Books for 2008* by *The Gulf Times, LoHud.com,* and *The Kansas City Star.* Paladin Contemporaries released her novels, *Hamburger Haven* (2009) and *Cicada Grove* (1992). She holds an MA in English/creative writing and a *Juris Doctor.*
"About Kansas City? It's home. Even if I'm constantly wanting to leave when I live there, I long for it when I live elsewhere."

Hilary Masters was born and grew up in Kansas City, Missouri. He is the author of twenty books, including *Post, a Fable* (BkMk Press, 2011), a memoir *Last Stands: Notes from Memory* (David Godine, 1982), and his third collection of short stories, *How the Indians Buried Their Dead* (Southern Methodist University Press, 2009), was honored by the Independent Publishers Association, with the so-called Ippy Award for Fiction. He is married to the mystery writer Kathleen George, and they live in Pittsburgh, Pa.
"My brief history in Kansas City has given me a treasury that has enriched my life and work."

Jo McDougall's publications include five books of poetry, the most recent being *Dirt* and *Satisfied with Havoc;* a 2010 chapbook, *Under an Arkansas Sky;* and a 2011 memoir, *Daddy's Money: a Memoir of Farm and Family.* A collection of new and selected poems is in progress.
"Kansas City fosters an amazing community of gifted, diverse writers that nourishes my writing life."

James McKinley has published two novels, three books of short fiction and two non-fiction books. After a stint in NYC advertising, he taught at UMKC for 34 years, the last seventeen serving as editor of *New Letters* magazine. Currently he is finishing a book of short stories, while working as a free-lance editor.

"Metropolitan Kansas City's rich culture – in performing arts, visual arts, jazz, sports and literary arts – merits a star above many larger cities."

Patricia Cleary Miller is the author of the local history, *Westport: Missouri's Port of Many Returns* (Lowell Press); the poetry collection *Starting A Swan Dive* (BkMk Press); the chapbook *Dresden* (Helicon Nine Editions); and the collection *Crimson Lights* (Covington). She teaches at Rockhurst University, where she edits the *Rockhurst Review.*

"My Kansas City roots date back to 1868 when my father's grandparents arrived from Ireland. Members of our family have lived in and loved the midtown area ever since. Our family home is full of story-telling treasures."

Philip Miller (1943 – 2011) graduated from Emporia Teachers College, taught at Kansas City, KS Community College, and was a founding member of The Writers Place. He started and directed the Riverfront Reading Series from 1987-2004. He is widely published and has seven books of poetry. He died on Valentine's Day in 2011, but his legacy for promoting poetry in Kansas City lives on.

Originally from Cincinnati, Ohio, **Wayne Miller** is the author of three poetry collections, most recently *The City, Our City* (Milkweed, 2011), which was a finalist for the William Carlos Williams Award and the Rilke Prize. Also an editor and a translator, Miller lives in Waldo and teaches at the University of Central Missouri, where he edits *Pleiades.*

"When I moved to Kansas City from Houston, Texas, in 2002, I was pleased to discover that Kansas City is, in fact, a real city interconnected with cities all over the world, flush with art and commerce, beautiful architecture, food, and (unfortunately) violence, and possessing of a striking number of extraordinary people. I had no idea what to expect when I arrived, and in many ways Kansas City has been a lovely surprise."

Al Ortolani is a teacher. His poetry has been accepted by journals such as *Prairie Schooner, New Letters,* and the *New York Quarterly.* He has three books of poetry, *The Last Hippie of Camp 50* and *Finding the*

Edge, published by Woodley Press and *Wren's House,* published by Coal City Press.

"When I was a boy, I used to ride the Kansas City Southern from Pittsburg to Kansas City with my grandmother. I was enthralled by Union Station, Woolworth's, and the smell of diesel from city buses. Fifty years later I'm still moved by a similar vibrancy."

Eve Ott's fiction and poetry have appeared or are forthcoming in *The Same, Imagination and Place, I-70 Review, Redbook, Thorny Locust, Rusty Truck, Rebirth of Power,* and various campus and regional publications. She is active in the Kansas City literary community as a member of The Riverfront Reading Series Committee and The Writers Place.

"I love Kansas City: the galleries, theater, music, restaurants, but most especially the vibrant writers' community and our wonderful venue for readings, The Writers Place."

David Owen has been a staff writer for *The New Yorker* since 1991. He has also been a contributing editor of *The Atlantic Monthly,* a senior writer for *Harper's,* and a contributing editor of *Golf Digest,* and he has written more than a dozen books. His wife and both their children are also writers, and they all love Kansas City.

H.C. Palmer is a retired Medical Doctor, Vietnam War Battalion Surgeon and poet. He is an assistant poetry editor for *Narrative Magazine.* A recent poem in *New Letters* was nominated for a Pushcart Prize and for *Best New Poets, 2012.*

"I believe the Kansas City area poetry community is outstanding and inspiring."

Anika Paris is a platinum award-winning singer/songwriter with songs in major films/television and Off-Broadway productions. Her poems appeared in *KC Star, Helicon Nine Editions, Gival Press, Half Shell Press, Scapegoat Press.* She teaches songwriting and performance at Musicians Institute in Hollywood with her new book *Making Your Mark in Music,* published by Hal Leonard.

"I spent my formative years growing up in Kansas City and to this day I miss the tree-lined skies."

Steve Paul, a senior writer and arts editor for *The Kansas City Star,* writes about books, music, the local arts scene, architecture and restaurants. His magazine feature "Architecture A-Z: An Elemental, Alphabetical Guide to the Built Environment" was published as a book in 2011. Steve is also editor of *Kansas City Noir* (Akashic Books, Brooklyn, 2012), and co-editor of an essay collection, *War & Ink: New Perspectives on Ernest Heming-way's Early Years*, forthcoming from The Kent State University Press in 2013.

Susan Peters grew up in Lawrence, Kansas and returned to her Midwestern roots in 2006, after working in Russia, China, Poland, Germany, and Mexico. Her poetry has appeared in *Kansas City Voices*, *Light Quarterly*, and *Lucidity*, as well as online in anderbo.com, *Persimmon Tree*, and *The Barefoot Muse*.
"I live in Kansas City because it has everything I love – great ethnic food (Thai, Salvadoran, Ethiopian), the world's best barbecue, dear friends, and work that's a constant joy."

Michael Pritchett is the author of *The Melancholy Fate of Capt. Lewis* (2007) and *The Venus Tree*, Iowa Short Fiction Award (1988) and winner of the 2000 Dana Award for *The Final Effort of the Archer*. His work has appeared in *The Iowa Award: The Best Stories from 20 Years* (1990), and in *Natural Bridge* and *New Letters* among others. He teaches at the University of Missouri-Kansas City.
"I've always liked the advice printed in an 1851 Indiana newspaper editorial to 'Go West, young man!' because it embodies the highest roman-tic ideal of the rugged, self-made American before it runs up against the Civil War, Little Big Horn, the Depression, Vietnam and 9/11. Kansas City is the place where the river essentially ends, or goes north, and the wagon trails west begin – which means it's been here all this time, as a witness to both the dream and reality of westward expansion. This makes the city a really interesting place for artists and historians to continue to bear witness to the evolution of a dream."

Alan R. Proctor wrote his first poem at age six and since then has published poetry and/or prose in *New Letters*, *Crosstimbers*, *The Red Book*, *Off Channel*, *Loon*, and *Kansas City Voices* among other journals. A retired fundraiser and avid classical guitarist, Alan and his wife, Susan, enjoy their 100-year-old home in Brookside and being able to walk to the grocers.

Kevin Rabas co-directs the creative writing program at Emporia State and edits *Flint Hills Review*. He has three books: *Bird's Horn*, *Lisa's Flying Electric Piano* (a Kansas Notable Book and Nelson Poetry Book Award winner), and *Spider Face: stories*. He writes regularly for KC's Jazz Ambassador Magazine (JAM).

"KC is one of the cradle places of jazz, one of the truly American, democratic art forms, and, as a teen, KC is one of the places I cut my musical teeth, in its jam sessions across the city."

David Ray's latest book is *Hemingway: A Desperate Life*. Other titles include *After Tagore* and *When*. *Music of Time: Selected & New Poems* offers selections from fifteen previous volumes, and *Sam's Book* has been re-released from Wesleyan University Press. An emeritus professor of the University of Missouri-Kansas City, where he also edited *New Letters* and founded *New Letters on the Air*, David now lives and writes in Tucson. (www.davidraypoet.com)

Judy Ray's poetry books include *To Fly Without Wings*, Helicon Nine Editions, and *Fishing in Green Waters*, Cervena Barva Press. While living in Kansas City, she was associate editor of *New Letters* and the first director of The Writers Place. Born and raised in England, she has lived in and written about many other parts of the world, and now makes her home in Tucson, Arizona.

Samuel Cyrus David Ray (1965 - 1984) was a student at Carleton College where he was killed in an accident. Although he lived most of the time in Minnesota, he spent time in Kansas City with his father and family. He was involved in college sports and also appreciated poetry. His favorite actor was Steve Martin, and one of his favorite books was *How To Be Loved*, an art at which he excelled.

Trish Reeves's books include *In the Knees of the Gods* (BkMk Press) and *Returning the Question* (which received the Cleveland State University Poetry Center Prize). She has received fellowships for her poetry from the National Endowment for the Arts, Yaddo, and Sarah Lawrence College. She leads the men and women's Changing Lives Through Literature seminars for Johnson County Corrections, and is a Kansas Humanities Scholar in Literature.
"Kansas City was my first big city, and I loved it because my grandmother lived here; making it my own home as an adult, I continue to love Kansas City, for many reasons, but, again, mostly because of the people I've come to know and love here – so many found in the remarkable community of poets, writers and editors."

Carl Rhoden lives in Lee's Summit, Missouri. He has published poems in *Rockhurst Review*, *I-70 Review*, *River King*, *Coal City Review*,

The Same, and other magazines. He was born in a log cabin in Kansas City, Missouri, during the heyday of Greek tragedy.

Richard Rhodes is the author of twenty-four books including *The Making of the Atomic Bomb,* which won a Pulitzer Prize in Nonfiction, a National Book Award and a National Book Critics Circle Award; *Dark Sun: The Making of the Hydrogen Bomb,* which was shortlisted for a Pulitzer Prize in History; a biography, *John James Audubon: The Making of an American;* a memoir of childhood, *A Hole in the World;* and a biography of Hedy Lamarr, *Hedy's Folly.* He has received fellowships from the Ford Foundation, the Guggenheim Foundation, the MacArthur Foundation, and the Alfred P. Sloan Foundation. With his wife, Dr. Ginger Rhodes, a clinical psychologist, he lives near Half Moon Bay, California.
"I was born and grew up in Kansas City; to this day it's never far from my thoughts."

Shirley Rickett's book *Love: Poems for Vintage Song Titles* is published by Finishing Line Press. Her poems also appear in journals such as *Smartish Pace, New Letters, Kaleidoscope,* and anthologies such as *Boundless, From A to Z,* and Missouri Poetry Society. A lifelong Kansas Citian, she and husband Charles retired to South Texas in the Rio Grande Valley where Rickett writes and sometimes teaches in the Pharr Literacy Project.

Judith Towse Roberts is an area writer, teacher of creative writing, and poet. She has published a book of poetry titled *Chrysanthemums I Once Thought Sweet* (Mid-America Press), which was a finalist in the Thorpe Menn competition. Her works have appeared in many literary magazines as well as *Chicken Soup for the Mother's Soul.*
"Known as the Heartland of this nation, Kansas City is a cultural Center for the Arts in the Midwest, and many celebrated writers, musicians, and artists have given Voice to this great city."

Andrés Rodríguez's poems have appeared in *New York Quarterly, Harvard Review, Cortland Review,* and several anthologies including *Wild Song* (University of Georgia Press). He is the author of *Night Song* (Tia Chucha Press) and *Book of the Heart* (Lindisfarne Press). In 2007 he won Poets & Writers' Maureen Egen Award.

Linda Rodriguez's *Every Last Secret* (Minotaur Books) won the Malice Domestic Best First Traditional Mystery Novel Competition, was selected by Las Comadres National Latina Book Club, and was a Barnes & Noble mystery pick. For her books of poetry, *Skin Hunger* (Potpourri Publications; Scapegoat Press) and *Heart's Migration* (Tia Chucha Press), Rodriguez received the Midwest Voices & Visions Award, Elvira Cordero Cisneros Award, and Thorpe Menn Award.

Elizabeth Rowe, PhD, M.B.A., is an expert in the thermodynamics of membranes and protein folding and has multiple scientific publications. She was raised in Seattle, Ohio, and Alabama, and educated at Duke and Georgetown Universities. In addition to being a scientist she is a horse woman, writer, pilot and sculptor.
"The juxtaposition of the wide open spaces of Kansas with a vibrant, diverse, modern city of a suitable size makes it a great place to raise kids and learn to fly."

Vernon Rowe is a neurologist, scientist-inventor, and writer. Previously published work appears in the medical literature, patents, and *Sea Creatures* and *The Ride*, collections of poems, prose, and one-act plays. Rowe was reared in the Appalachian mountains of North Carolina, attended Duke and Johns Hopkins, and heads the Rowe Neurology Institute and Verrow, Inc., located in Lenexa, KS.

Ann Slegman is a writer and editor in Kansas City. Her novel, *Return to Sender*, and her collection of poems, *Conversation*, were published by Helicon Nine Editions.

Mbembe Milton Smith (1946-1982) was in the first class of students at the University of Missouri-Kansas City to get an M.A. in English with an emphasis in creative writing. He published four books of poems, and a posthumous *Selected Poems* was published by BkMk Press. He thought of himself as a black writer writing for a black audience. He taught at Rockhurst College, Fordham University, and in the City University of New York system. Shortly after moving to Chicago in 1982 he took his life. His work has gone on to garner praise and attention.

Bob Sommer is the author of *Where the Wind Blew: A Novel* (2008) and *A Great Fullness*, forthcoming from Aqueous Books. He is currently writing a memoir about his family's experience of a decade of American war. He blogs at *Uncommon Hours* and invites visitors to his son's memorial website: www.francisfund.org.

"A couple fashion tips I picked up living in Kansas City for twenty-four years: don't wear a suit to Arthur Bryant's and do flaunt my Yankees cap at The K."

Robert Stewart's *Outside Language: Essays* was a finalist for a PEN Center USA Award. He is executive editor for BkMk Press and *New Letters on the Air*, and editor of *New Letters* at the University of Missouri-Kansas City. He won a 2008 National Magazine Award from the American Society of Magazine Editors.
"The generosity, good will, and passion of people in the Kansas City literary community have been the nurturing elements of any talent I might have developed over the years."

Polly W. Swafford taught for 27 years in the Shawnee Mission Public School District. In 1989 she co-founded *Potpourri: A Magazine of the Literary Arts* and later become publisher for Potpourri Publications until retiring in 2004. Her award-winning works have appeared in numerous publications and her chapbook of haiku, *Early Freeze*, was published in 2010.
"Kansas City is really a mecca for lovers of the arts – literary, visual or performing. What a gift that one can find outstanding arts programs every day of the week in our metro area!"

James Tate, born in Kansas City, has a long list of award-winning books to his name, including *The Lost Pilot*, Yale Series of Younger Poets, 1967, and *Selected Poems*, Wesleyan University Press, 1991, for which he received the Pulitzer Prize in Poetry. He teaches at the University of Massachusetts, Amherst, and is a Chancellor of the Academy of American Poets.

Alarie Tennille serves on the Board of Directors of The Writers Place in Kansas City, Missouri. Her chapbook, *Spiraling into Control*, is available on Amazon.com. Alarie's poems have appeared in numerous journals including *Margie, Poetry East, English Journal, I-70 Review, Wild Goose Poetry Review*, and *Untitled Country Review*.
"Researching possible retirement locales has made me appreciate how rare it is to have the supportive writing community I've found in Kansas City."

Whitney Terrell is the author of *The Huntsman*, a *New York Times* notable book, and *The King of Kings County*, which was selected as a best book of 2005 by *The Christian Science Monitor*. His non-fiction has appeared in *The New York Times, The Washington Post, Slate*, and on

National Public Radio. He is the *New Letters* Writer in Residence at UMKC.

Author of fifteen books and two children, **Roderick Townley** is known for his novels for young readers, including *The Great Good Thing* and *The Door in the Forest*. He has published two volumes of poetry and won many honors, the greatest of which is his marriage to poet Wyatt Townley. (www.rodericktownley.com)
"Something about Kansas City, its feeling of openness and possibility, has helped this New York refugee make a vow never to write a book he wouldn't want to read."

Wyatt Townley's work has been read by Garrison Keillor on NPR, featured by Ted Kooser in his poetry column, and published in journals ranging from *The Paris Review* to *Newsweek*. Her latest book is *The Afterlives of Trees*, completed with a fellowship from the Kansas Arts Commission and selected as a Kansas Notable Book. (www.WyattTownley.com)
"Kansas City is still an open secret – from its location straddling two states to the unexpected depth and breadth of its arts community."

William Trowbridge's latest poetry collection is *Ship of Fool* (Red Hen Press, 2011). His other collections are *The Complete Book of Kong*, *Flickers*, *O Paradise*, and *Enter Dark Stranger*. He lives in the Kansas City area and teaches in the University of Nebraska Low-residency MFA in Writing Program. In April, 2012, he was appointed to a two-year term as Poet Laureate of Missouri.

Donna Trussell's collection of poems, *What's Right About What's Wrong*, won the Thorpe Menn Award in 2009. Her short stories have appeared in *TriQuarterly*, *North American Review* and other journals, and her essays have appeared *The Kansas City Star*, *Politics Daily* and *The Washington Post*. Born in Texas, she has lived in Kansas City since 1977.

Leslie Ullman has published three poetry collections, and her fourth will appear in 2013 from University of New Mexico Press. Professor Emerita at University of Texas-El Paso, she is a faculty member in the low-residency MFA Program at Vermont College of the Fine Arts. She lives in Taos, New Mexico.

Gloria Vando's poetry has won numerous awards, including the Di Castagnola Award, Latino Literary Hall of Fame's Poetry Book Award, Thorpe Menn Award. A new book, *Woven Voices* (Scapegoat Press, 2012) is a compilation of poems by 3 generations: Vando's mother, Anita Velez-Mitchell, her daughter, Anika Paris, and herself. She is publisher/editor of Helicon Nine Editions and co-founder of The Writers Place.
"Kansas City is a haven for poets and writers. The literary community is inclusive, supportive, and nurturing."

Maryfrances Wagner's books include *Salvatore's Daughter* (BkMk), *Red Silk* (MidAm, winner of the Thorpe Menn Book Award), and *Light Subtracts Itself* (MidAm). Poems have appeared in *New Letters*, *Midwest Quarterly*, *Laurel Review*, *Voices in Italian Americana*, *Unsettling America: An Anthology of Contemporary Multicultural Poetry* (Penguin Books), *Literature Across Cultures* (Pearson/Longman), *Bearing Witness* (Zephyr) and *The Dream Book* (winner of the American Book Award from Before Columbus Foundation).
"Kansas City continues to produce and nurture good writers, and many of them keep their connections to a city that remains a great place to live and a great place to experience culture across all arts and genres."

Sylvia Griffith Wheeler (1930 – 2012) published numerous award-winning works of poetry and creative writing. She was a native Kansan, received an MFA from University of Missouri-Kansas City, and was a Professor of English at the University of South Dakota.
Sylvia found inspiration with fellow Midwestern writers in graduate school in the 1960s at UMKC. She loved the energy, creativeness, and friendships she made in readings around Kansas City in the 1960s and 70s.

Susan Whitmore is the author of *The Sacrifices* (Mellen Poetry Press 1990) and *The Melinda Poems* (Pudding House Press 2004). Her work has recently appeared in the *Georgetown Review*, *CrossCurrents*, *Georgia Review* and *New Letters*, among others.
"I was transplanted from the East Coast to the Midwest 20 years ago. Kansas City poetics, to me, melds bovine beauty with the beat of the jazz greats."

Jeanie Wilson's book of poetry is *Uncurling* (Mid-America Press, 2000). The Kansas Library Association and the Kansas State School for the Visually Handicapped sponsored a statewide exhibit (1983-1986) of her poetry and photography. She was awarded the Barbara

Storck Creative Writing Award in 1990. She has served as Director of Field Services for Educational Systems at The University of Kansas, training teachers nation-wide.

Thomas Zvi Wilson (1931 – 2012), a visual artist and poet, has been published and anthologized widely. His first book, *Deliberate and Accidental Acts* (BkMk Press) was a Thorpe Menn Book Award finalist. In 2000, he co-authored *The Door into the Dream* with his wife Jeanie. He started the Writers Place Poetry Reading Series at the Jo Co Central Resource Library and served as Writers Place board member and treasurer. He died of a rare neurological condition in 2012.

Janice Funk Yocum teaches creative writing at a Charter School, Lee A. Tolbert Community Academy. She has a B.A. in Education from the University of Missouri—Columbia and an M.A. from U.M.K.C. She has published poems in several literary magazines and has been widely praised for publication and presentation of her students' work.